RSS-BJP

TOWARDS KASHMIR, ARAB-ISRAEL CONFLICT & BANGLADESH

RSS-BJP

TOWARDS KASHMIR, ARAB-ISRAEL CONFLICT & BANGLADESH

Prof. Ram Sakal Singh

Manas Publications
(We Convert Fighters into Writers)
New Delhi - 110 002 (INDIA)

MANAS PUBLICATIONS
(We Convert Fighters into Writers)
(Publishers, Library Suppliers, Importers & Exporters)
4402/5-A, Ansari Road (Opp. HDFC Bank)
Darya Ganj, New Delhi - 110 002 (India)
Phones: Off.: 011-23260783, 23265523, Res.: 011-23842660
E-mail: manaspublications@gmail.com
manaspublications@yahoo.com
Website: www.manaspublications.in

ISBN 978-81-7049-514-7

₹ 595.00

Designed at
Manas Publications

Printed in India at
R.K. Printers, Delhi
and published by Mrs Suman Lata for
Manas Publications, 4402/5-A,
Ansari Road (Opp HDFC Bank),
Darya Ganj, New Delhi - 110002 (INDIA)

To

my mother

Late SHANTI DEVI

and

my father

Late MAHADEO SINGH

whose honesty and integrity are
symbol of my progress.

Foreword

Emergence of Jana Sangh and its evolution as the Bharatiya Janata Party (BJP) as a national political party of India is the result of current of opposition against the Indian National Congress in the realm of Indian party politics. The Indian National Congress having its political background during the freedom struggle of India where it achieved wide appreciation and all round admiration remained a dominant political party all over the country till 1967 when other political parties either regional or national appeared as a force to reckon with. However, the history of Jana Sangh is different. Its leaders lacked reputation as freedom fighters and it came into existence soon after the advent of the Indian Constitution and began to play the role in Indian parliamentary politics. The early leaders of the RSS having strong national sentiments played remarkable role in the rise and growth of Jana Sangh. It was very much critical to the domestic as well as external policies of the Congress party under the leadership of Pandit Jawaharlal Nehru. So long as Pandit Nehru dominated the political scene of India, no party including Jana Sangh replaced the Congress from power. After Nehru's death, political scenario of India began to change fast paving the emergence of growth of other political parties. The Jana Sangh leaders availed this opportunity to strengthen its ground adopting ideologies like national integration, protection of ancient Indian culture and civilization, establishment of Hindu Dharma Rajya, strong foreign policy, protecting the Indian interests abroad and a powerful effective

India to meet the challenges extended by neighbouring inimical countries of India like Pakistan and China. It rejected faith in policy of non-alignment and liberal attitude towards enemy nations. Its inclination towards Hindu nation created doubt in the mind of secular forces and enabled them to propagate Jana Sangh as a party of Hindus. However, the leaders of Jana Sangh tried best to remove such apprehensions from the minds of people, both inside and outside the country, advancing the logic that the party stands for strong India and Indianisation, but not against any particular community.

Strength of Jana Sangh began to get enlarged after the change of its nomenclature as the BJP. It availed the opportunity to form government at Centre in the coalition government under the dominant and seasoned politician of BJP, namely Atal Bihari Vajpayee. He successfully managed to remain in power for full tenure, no doubt, but he failed to block the way to the Congress in coming years. It is all because of emergence of coalition system in the Indian politics and also re-emergence of the strength of Congress under the leadership and supervision of Sonia Gandhi who took all the troubles to improve the position of Congress. The party remained in power for two complete tenures, no doubt, but disunity among the coalition government of Dr Manmohan Singh and involvement of the Congress as well as other coalition partners in mass corruption prepared ground for demolition of the Congress party and coalition government. The Indian electorate once again expressed their absolute faith in the BJP which has declared Narendra Modi, the then Chief Minister of Gujarat, as would-be Prime Minister of India. The charismatic personality and magic of Modi-chanting people with the result that the BJP emerged as ruling party having absolute majority to form the government. Presently Modi government is working hard to improve the lot of India and its people. The people of India are expecting a lot from Modi and his government. For the first time BJP has availed the full majority to give practical shape to the ideology and its policies and programmes. Remarkable changes are expected in India under the leadership of Narendra Modi. If the party fails to achieve the declared as well as decided goals, it would definitely be very difficult for BJP to emerge as a ruling party of the country.

Prof Ram Sakal Singh, a renowned scholar who has published a number of research articles and books, have applied sincere efforts to present the picture of Jana Sangh right from its origin to evolution as a national party called Bharatiya Janata Party (BJP). He has critically analysed the facts related to the working of the Party in the interest of India. In that sense Prof Ram Sakal Singh has thoroughly investigated and critically examined the events related to Indian politics, both domestic and foreign. His special emphasis has been to explore and discuss the sentiments and attitude of BJP leaders towards Kashmir, Bangladesh, Arabian countries and Israel. In my opinion this book, presented by Prof Ram Sakal Singh, is a good contribution to understand BJP and its political activities including Indian party politics.

Chandrika Singh
Retired Professor and Head
Department of Political Science
Nagaland Central University
Lumami, Mokokchung

Preface

Prime Minister Narendra Modi's Japan visit was full of specific purposes. He tried to encourage the government and industrialists of Japan to make investment in the economic field of India and got success. Shinzo Abe, the Prime Minister of Japan agreed to help India in bringing Bullet train. He also agreed to invest $ 35 billion in India in the gradual process to improve Indian economic infrastructure and develop economic system. His journey to Japan is also a milestone for both the countries. He succeeded in making Japan a reliable and close friend of India. First time after independence, the Government of India, under the leadership of Narendra Modi, brought Japan very close to India. The meeting of Narendra Modi with the Japanese Prime Minister Shinzo Abe attracted attention of the world providing India a respectable place in international politics.

When the Chinese President Xi Jinping visited India, Modi spared nothing to win over the heart of the Chinese President and people of China. He assured China that India, as neighbour of China, having big market would help China in its economic growth. However, he made it clear that India's relationship with China would not be durable until the prolonged border dispute is resolved amicably. Chinese President Xi Jinping agreed with Modi and assured him to maintain peace on border line between both the countries. While giving heartfelt welcome and honour to Chinese President,

Modi successfully reduced the tension between India and China. Chinese President assured India to make investment in the industrial field, specially in railways with the purpose to enable India to start Bullet train, the most valuable dream of the Indian Prime Minister Narendra Modi.

Prime Minister Narendra Modi and Chinese President Xi Jinping signed 12 agreements. China will help India in the development of railways. China will invest $ 20,000 crore in India during five years. In September 2014, Narendra Modi visited America on five days' trip. In America he attended at least fifty-five meetings and impressed people too much. The American visit of Indian Prime Minister attracted the attention of the world. Warm welcome and reception was given to him in the Madison Square building. This was unique and unprecedented. There was no space in the Madison Square to accommodate the people gathered outside. Standing outside the Madison Square building, public listened his speech attentively. Their echoing proved that Modi was their hero. It helped to bring India and USA closer. His meeting with Barak Obama was held in very cordial atmosphere. Obama liked Modi and discussed with him international affairs. Both the leaders agreed to deal with some vexed international problems jointly such as the discussion of growing international terrorism, emergence of dictatorial forces in some Islamic countries at the cost of democracy. Several agreements were signed between US and India related to economic development, expansion of atomic energy, investment of capital for the development of new industries and manufacturing, joint practice of naval as well as air forces etc. Both the nations took vow to work unitedly for eradication of terrorists from the world and to rescue people from mounting attacks of terror forces.

Addressing the UN General Assembly, Narendra Modi made it amply clear that time has come to make the UN more strong, effective and useful in the interest of the whole world. He also said that new outlook and vision is required to enable the UN to meet new challenges and fulfil the hopes of the people of the world. On Pakistan, Narendra Modi explicitly said,

> "I am prepared to engage in a serious bilateral dialogue with Pakistan in a peaceful atmosphere, without the shadow of terrorism, to promote our friendship and cooperation. However, Pakistan must also take its responsibility seriously to create an appropriate environment for it. Raising issues in this forum will derail the efforts to resolve the issues between our two countries."

It was a befitting reply to Pakistan with a sort of warning. Narendra Modi told the delegates of the UN that India believed in the principles of justice and universal brotherhood. India has no policy of expansionism rather it likes to maintain friendly as well as cooperative relations with neighbouring countries, whether they are big or small, powerful or powerless. India stands for equity among nations honouring their dignity. India also likes to honour the sovereignty of other nations. Thus the vision of Prime Minister Narendra Modi to USA and his address in the UN added honour and dignity of India, both abroad and inside the country. Modi has become the national hero in the international arena, he is emerging as a rock star. It appears that some notable changes are taking place in the field of foreign affairs, economic activities, diplomatic policies and political activities.

As Prime Minister of India, Narendra Modi has established his reputation all over the country. The people of India are expecting a lot from such a visionary prime minister. In fact, Narendra Modi was trying to achieve the lost image and dignity of India. He wants to make India united, powerful, strong and respectable. Within few months of his rule he launched some projects for the development of India and its people. For the first time, with the help of Indian banks he encouraged Indian masses to open bank accounts with zero balance under Jan-Dhan Yojana on the eve of Mahatma Gandhi birthday (2nd October 2014). Modi launched Clean India Mission (स्वच्छ भारत अभियान), he encouraged people including leaders, politicians and bureaucrats to make India free from garbage. He also asked people to sweep each and every road, streets etc. Due to his initiative and encouragement people not only took trouble to sweep out darts with the help of brooms; but also took vow to keep India clean and bright.

In the field of economic development he is trying hard to reduce the price of petrol and diesel. Prices of petrol and diesel are coming down, which has given some economic relief to the people. Modi is planning to control corruption which has entered in all aspects of human life of India. He is constantly instructing his ministers and bureaucrats to be honest and work with dedication and commitment to the service of the nation and the people. He instructed each Member of Parliament to adopt one village in his area for making it an ideal village.

Thus Modi has become the symbol of hope and aspiration of the people of India. Even at the international level, small and big nations are expecting from Modi to improve international politics. Modi is always ready to help the distressed people suffering from droughts, floods and other natural calamities, for instance, he sanctioned crores of rupees to help the people of Jammu and Kashmir, who were suffering from unexpected flood. He sanctioned ₹ 5 lakh to each victim of 1984 anti-Sikh riots, broke out after the death of Indira Gandhi. He declared 31st October to be celebrated as National Unity Day (राष्ट्रीय एकता दिवस) all over the country in honour of Sardar Vallabhbhai Patel. He is emerging as national hero. Under his leadership BJP won the assembly elections of Haryana and Maharashtra. This clearly proved that the magic of Modi is increasing, not decreasing in India. Modi has become universal national slogan. In the people's gathering echo of "Modi, Modi, Modi ..." has become a popular feature.

Prime Minister Narendra Modi-led government is coming up with new initiatives and programmes in its endeavour to boost the Indian economy. Ministers of the BJP government said they are all for reforms and economic growth, and that they would keep pursuing it in the Narendra Modi tenure.

Union Minister Piyush Goyal said,

> "Even if Congress keeps obstructing GST Bill, there would be other ways to deal with the situation.... We may have to look at alternative mechanisms to achieve the same goal."

Finance Minister Arun Jaitley said,

> "The government is working to enhance public expenditure in physical, social and rural infrastructure to push economic growth 1.5 percentage points higher than the 7-7.5% expected for the current financial year.

According to PwC (PricewaterhouseCoopers) report,

> "Of the emerging economies, only India is expected to grow faster in 2016 than its long-term average growth rate.... India will be a 'star performer' among emerging market economies and is expected to clock 7.7% growth in 2016, outshining China for the second consecutive year."

PwC report further noted that India will continue to reap the benefits of recent reforms. World Bank has projected that India would comfortably remain the fastest growing economy in 2016, at a rate more than a percentage point higher than that of China. The International Monetary Fund (IMF) believes that India is expected to grow by 7.3% this fiscal year and 7.5% in 2016-17.

India has taken the title of the world's fastest growing

economy from China. India's leadership holds unique impacts for the global economy and markets helping to buffer global weakness. Growth in India is set to outpace China for years to come. India will need to create 100 million new jobs over the next 10 years. For perspective, that is two-thirds of the size of the entire civilian labour force in the United States.

India is a services and consumer-driven economy looking to step up spending on infrastructure and boost manufacturing output. Prime Minister Modi is focused on reforms intended to simplify regulatory red tape, make the business environment friendlier to foreign firms, develop the nation's infrastructure, and build an educated workforce. India's service sector strength can help to offset some of the global weakness in manufacturing. Also, India's rising demand for construction is helping to offset some of the weakness in global commodity demand. India's rising growth helps to paint a brighter global economic outlook. In the near-term, interest rate cuts by the central bank combined with government infrastructure spending is helping to boost growth in India.

From the World Bank to Goldman Sachs had predicted it wouldn't happen for another two years but recent recalculations indicate that India has already dethroned China as the world's fastest-growing big economy.

Modi's plan for overall development of the masses, right from the down-trodden, will definitely help BJP to emerge as a major political force at the national level. In future, BJP will become the lifeline of Indian politics and will earn a respectable place in the hearts of the people.

I am thankful to Manas Publications, New Delhi, who agreed to publish this book.

Ram Sakal Singh

Contents

CHAPTER 1

Introduction

Theoretical Background

A political party is regarded as an enduring and legitimate instrument for the attainment of people's political objectives. It is truly the lifeline of modern politics.

There was a time in human history when political parties were looked down upon as creators of disunity in the people, and therefore, hampering nation-building. It is for this reason that George Washington in his farewell address warned the American people against formation of political parties.[1]

The political parties thus suffered from a stigma in popular estimation, which was gradually discarded. Political parties came to be recognized through a devious course.[2]

Walpole in England made systematic efforts to secure majority support for his government in Parliament by paying each member at the end of each session. Thus, it is through such methods that Parliamentary groupings came into shape.

Edmund Burke gave a new perspective to these groupings and attached some respectability to them. He renamed these groups as parties and characterized them as being public-spirited organizations. Political parties today have come to be regarded as the wheel of democracy and they owe their recognition as such to the influence of Burke's ideas. A modern political theorist regards political party as "a social formation which serves as social reservoir for the collection of a set of connected ideas from the area of voluntary society, and also (to) serve as a political conduit or channel by which the idea connected from that area flow from their social reservoir into the system of the state and turn the wheels of political machinery in that system."[3] The functions of political parties may be said to be: to borrow Almond and Coleman; interest articulation, interest aggregation, political socialization and training and political communication.[4]

Other functions of political parties is to legitimize the authority of the government by winning and sustaining popular support for the government.[5]

Importance of the Subject

Political parties thus play a vital role in the functioning of democracy. They are the hub of democracy and both are inseparable. They work "with a view of capture political power and to exercise it,"[6] including the formulation and implementation of foreign policy of the country.

Foreign policy of a country is formally determined by its government but the government is not totally free in this regard. A nation's foreign policy is the pursuit of its national interests, in perception and identification of national interests of views and reactions of other political parties in the country.

In this way, foreign policy is in its reality a result of interaction of different political forces operating in the country. They reflect not only the attitude of the ruling party but also, to some extent at least, the views and attitudes of the opposition parties. In case of irreconcilable difference, the opposition parties try to change the official policy by criticizing and attacking it in parliamentary and other forums and they seek to mould public opinion in support of their stand. Thus, the views and attitude of the political parties find their reflection to some extent in their attitudes towards issues of foreign policy.

Study of interaction between principles and ideologies of the political parties and their attitudes towards issues of foreign policy is of great importance not for a proper appreciation of foreign policy, but also for the democratic process involved.

An opposition party of today may be a ruling party tomorrow. "The opposition," said Prof Jennings, "is at once the alternative government and a focus for the discontent of the people. Its functions are almost as important as that of the government,"[7] and even the views of a ruling party today are often coloured and conditioned by the attitude and criticism of opposition parties. Therefore, a study of the interaction between principles and ideologies of an opposition political party and its attitudes towards issues of foreign policy is of great importance for understanding the political process in the country.

Purpose and Method of the Present Investigation

The purpose of the present investigation is to study the attitude and views of Bharatiya Jana Sangh, a national political party of India, towards India's foreign policy with special reference to the Arab-Israel conflict, Kashmir and Bangladesh.

Study of this problem would naturally involve a discussion of principles, ideologies as well as policies and programmes of the party as a necessary prelude to the discussion of the main problem.

I carry out this investigation and main reliance has been put on library research supplemented by interviews with some of the prominent leaders of Bharatiya Jana Sangh and some other political parties. I particularly consulted the Parliamentary debates and the back volumes of the *Organiser*.

Review of Literature

Political parties have become centre of political activities. This has naturally attracted attention of authors and research scholars. Therefore, numerous studies have been made for Indian political parties from different angles.[8]

Myron Weiner's pioneer study, *Party Building in a New Nation: The Indian National Congress*, SA Kochanek's *The Congress Party of India: The Dynamics of a One Party Democracy*, Richard Sisson's *The Congress Party in Rajasthan: Political Integration and Institution-Building in an Indian State* are among the important studies made on the Congress Party in India. Studies have also been made on Jana Sangh. Among them Craig Baxter's *The Jana Sangh: A Biography of an Indian Political Party* and MA Jhangiani's *Jana Sangh* and *Swatantra: A Profile of the Rightist Parties in India* and Mohammed Ali Kishore's *Jana Sangh and India's Foreign Policy*.

In this connection two books are particularly worth mentioning. One is the *Jana Sangh: A Biography of an Indian Political Party* by Craig Baxter.[9] And the other is *Jana Sangh and India's Foreign Policy* by Mohammed Ali Kishore.[10] The first is a biographical study of the Jana Sangh and is useful for a comprehensive history and analysis of the electoral performance of the party in the four General Elections held in 1952, 1957, 1962 and 1969. It does not deal with the attitude of the Jana Sangh on foreign policy matters.

Kishore's book is more relevant. It seeks to examine the foreign policy of Jana Sangh in general. It deals with the Kashmir till 1968 and devotes three bare pages on Israel. The Bangladesh problem had not yet issued the magnitude which followed in later years after the publication of this book.

The present study is likely to throw significant inquests in understanding of interaction between domestic factors and foreign policy and the political process of formulation and implementation of the foreign policy of India. It will also show how attitudes of a political party on issues of foreign policy are influenced by its ideological commitment.

References

1. Richard Hofstadter: *The Idea of a Party System* (Scientific Book Agency, Calcutta, 1972), pp 90 ff.
2. J Friedrich: *Constitutional Government and Democracy* (New Delhi, Oxford and IBH, 1974), p 430 ff.
3. Earnest Barker: *Principles of Social and Political Theory* (Oxford University Press, 1961), p 210.
4. GA Almond and GB Powell: *Comparative Politics—A Developmental Approach* (New Delhi, Amerind Publishing Co, 1972), pp 121-27.
5. Myron Weiner and Joslaw Palombara (eds): *Political Parties and Political Development* (Princeton University Press, 1966), pp 400-420.
6. Gurumukh Nihal Singh: *The Changing Concept of Citizenship* (Bombay, Orient Longmans, 1958), p 188.
7. Ivor Jennings: *Cabinet Government* (Cambridge, Cambridge University Press, 1959), p 15.
8. Cf Horst Hart Mann: *Political Parties in India: Rajni Kothari's Politics in India* and AS Burger's *Opposition in a Dominant Party System*, etc.
9. Craig Baxter: *The Jana Sangh: A Biography of an Indian Political Party* (Bombay, Oxford University Press, 1971).
10. Muhammad Ali Kishore: *Jana Sangh and India's Foreign Policy* (New Delhi, Associated Publishing House, 1969).

CHAPTER 2

Genesis and Growth of the Bharatiya Jana Sangh

The Bharatiya Jana Sangh was established in 1951. It was formed, according to its former Secretary, to provide a forum for giving a "modern political expression of that national self which has been trying to manifest itself after a period of bondage of thousands of years." Two elements contributed towards its formation "an organization called the Rashtriya Swayamsevak Sangh (RSS) and a personality named Syama Prasad Mukherjee."[1] A large section of the workers of the RSS wanted a leader to guide them at the political party. Thus, the Jana Sangh was the result of an informal co-operation between a party without a leader and a leader without a party.

Naturally Jana Sangh derived some of its spiritual inspiration and ideological moorings as well as much its organizational base from the RSS.

According to a pronounced critic of the party,

> "The Jana Sangh was set up with the implicit understanding that the organisation will be manned and controlled by men deputed for the purpose by the RSS High Command although each can disown any link or association with the other."[2]

The subject of link between the RSS and the Jana Sangh has been a subject of continuing controversy and it did not die out even after the merger of the Jana Sangh into the Janata Party effected on 1 May 1977.

The Rashtriya Swayamsevak Sangh was founded by Dr Keshav Baliram Hedgewar in Nagpur in 1925 to revitalize the Hindus community. It was militant but non-political organization of the Hindus, primarily of youth, which acquired great strength and force through its emphasis on character, discipline, leadership and devotion to Unity of India. By 1948, it claimed 50,00,000 supporters, with 5,00,000 as its regular members.[3]

In the words of Dr VP Varma,

> "Dr Hedgewar believed that Hindustan belonged to Hindus. He wanted to hold proclamation of this doctrine of 'Hinducha Hindustan'."[4]

As the RSS has been the inspirer and sustainer of the Jana Sangh, an analysis in some detail of the principles and ideology of RSS is called for its bearing on the ideology of Hindu Rashtra. Madhav Sadashiv Golwalkar in his book *Why Rashtra* has observed,

> "Bharatiya Rashtra is an Hindu Rashtra historically, this is a Hindu Rashtra, which has been existing here from very ancient times. Hence freedom of land of the Bharat is the freedom of Hindu Rashtra. Prosperity of Bharat means establishment of the Hindu Rashtra in the world as a respectable entity."[5]

RSS believes that only the Hindus can have true love for this country. Golwalkar argued,

> "Non-Hindus are incapable of having any love for this land. Non-Hindus came as invaders to destroy us to establish their own supremacy."[6]

This line of thinking leads RSS to conclude that the real

national work is that which is done for furthering the interest of Hindus. Any action detrimental to the cause of Hindus of *ipso facto* anti-national. Hindus are the natural patriots.

These ideas of the RSS have influenced and conditioned the thinking of the Jana Sangh from its very inception, but instead of standing for Hindu Rashtra and Hindu culture the Jana Sangh says that it stands for 'Bharatiya Sanskriti' and 'Maryada'. As Dr Syama Prasad Mukherjee declared in 1951,

> "Our Party firmly believes that the future of Bharat lies in the proper appreciation and application of 'Bharatiya Sanskriti' and 'Maryada', while we, therefore aim at establishing Dharma Rajya or Rule of law, we only abide by the highest traditions of 'Bharatiya Sanskriti'."[7]

Jana Sangh also emphasizes the importance of what it called integral humanism. This was to be the corner stone of the entire Indian system. It tries to strike a balance between spiritualism and materialism and declared that,

> "There can be no spiritual salvation without material prosperity."[8]

Thus, both RSS and Jana Sangh stand for Hindu revivalism, whose main characteristics are as follows:

- It has romantic longing for the glory of the past Hindu culture "as opposed to the individualistic, critical, rationalistic and materialistic trends. Hindu revivalism stands for a traditional organic and associative outlook."[9]
- It emphasizes greater conformity to religion.
- Secondly, it believes that political and economic policy should be consistent with the Philosophy of Hinduism. In fact, "nationalism is vehicle for the crystallization of the cultural ascendancy of Hinduism."[10]

- It is opposed to socialism and sanctifies non-intervention of state in the economic life of the people. The Jana Sangh says that democracy is to be established not only in the political field but also in the social and political fields. The Jana Sangh regards scientific socialism propounded by Karl Marx as basically materialism and so inadequate.[11]
- Jana Sangh thinks that in practice, "socialism also leads to totalitarian state of the monolithic type, a Socialist State becomes a slave state, and if socialism does bring about equality, it is equality in slavery and serfdom."[12]
- The RSS opposed the partition of India and rendered great service to the refugees who migrated from Pakistan and India. In the wake of partition of India, in 1948 Mahatma Gandhi was murdered by a Maharashtrian and it was alleged that he had connections with the RSS and the Hindu Mahasabha. Within a few of days Gandhiji's murder, both these organizations were banned by the government on 4 February 1948, and their leaders were arrested. On 12 November 1949 the ban on RSS was removed.

It was during this period that a reappraisal took place among RSS leaders and the rank and file about the RSS attitude towards participation in active politics in the sense of contesting elections and entering legislatures. They felt that "had they been a large political force with representation in Parliament, it would not have been possible for the government to ban them,"[13] nor the government would have taken so long to lift the ban. They felt that their "influence had not been translated into legislative power, and as a result, the Congress Party used the assassination of Gandhi by a member of the Hindu Mahasabha as an opportunity to suppress the RSS and intern its leaders."[14] They also found, to their chagrin, that no substantial group in the Parliament rose to defend what they felt to be their most legitimate activities. Thus, many leaders of the RSS, of the rank and file, were psychologically prepared to reverse their attitude towards their active participation in politics and elections. They viewed the Hindu Mahasabha to be hopelessly discredited and ineffective party and considered its outlook to be very backward-looking rendering the party to be doomed beyond redemption. Hence, they needed for an independent party. They had considerable mass strength to build a political party. Further, many of the RSS people came to believe that, had they been in politics earlier, partition might not have occurred. They believed that social and cultural work was not enough to bring the adoption of this cultural form in the whole country.

> "Unity to country, for it was the political people, the Congress especially, who had partitioned the country and destroyed its political unity. This contrast between their mass strength and their political weakness, forcibly presented to them by the government ban, activated the RSS members in north India to enter politics."[15]
>
> (Richard D Lambert, "Hindu Communal Groups in Indian Politics", in Richard L Park and Irene Tinker (eds), *Leadership and Political Institutions in India* (Madras, Oxford University Press, 1960), p 211.)

On the other hand, Dr Syama Prasad Mukherjee was not finding himself reconciled with the outlook and policy of the Hindu Mahasabha and particularly after the assassination of Mahatma Gandhi he had proposed that the Mahasabha should leave politics and confine its activities to social and cultural fields like the Arya Samaj, or alternatively, should open its membership to the non-Hindu citizens of India as well. This was not acceptable to the Mahasabha and he resigned from it. In 1946 elections, Dr Mukherjee was elected to the

Constituent Assembly of India, and a year later joined the first Nehru cabinet as Minister of Industry and Supplies. He resigned from the Nehru Cabinet on the question of relations with Pakistan, and particularly the plight of the Hindu refugees from east Bengal in April 1950. Dr Mukherjee was thus, a leader without a political party after his resignation from the Hindu Mahasabha. Naturally, he was in "quest for a political platform."[16] He was very much impressed with the discipline and work of the RSS. Vasant Rao Oak, a leading RSS member, had discussed the organization of a new political party with Dr Mukherjee as early as 1949. In 1950, Oak assured Dr Mukherjee that if the latter resigned from the Nehru Cabinet to start a new political party, many of the RSS workers would powerfully support him.

Thus the situation was propitious for launching a new political party by the informal co-operation of a party without a leader and a leader without a party. When Dr Mukherjee resigned from Nehru Cabinet, the event was celebrated in Delhi. Several RSS leaders like VR Oak, Deendayal Upadhyaya, Dr Bhai Mahavir, Balraj Madhok and others took the initiative and were joined by several like-minded non-RSS personalities including Pandit DP Mishra, PB Gole, ex-ministers of the then Central Provinces, Balraj Mauli Chandra Sharma and Mahashaya Krishna.[17] Guruji Golwalkar, the Chief of the RSS, was frequently consulted, but he was neither enthused about nor against the proposal to start a new political party.[18] In 1946 elections, while a few individual Swayamsevaks of RSS participated in the elections, the RSS as a whole did not participate. On 10 November 1949, Golwalkar said at Ahmedabad, "We have forgotten that politics is only a part and parcel of the comprehensive life. Life is higher and wider than politics. The ritual component of life is not politics but culture. To regard political as all comprehensive is to abandon the soul of Bharat."[19] He was not prepared to officially endorse any

Political party but it was reported in the press by a source. "In intimate touch with inner developments" with RSS, which thought that the RSS would not take any initiative to form a new political party, but it would not with hold support to members of RSS who may form a new political party.[20] A conference of political workers was held in Calcutta in May 1951 to inaugurate the people's party in West Bengal under the presidentship of Dr Syama Prasad Mukherjee.[21] A few weeks later, it was reported that about 250 workers from Punjab, and Himachal Pradesh met at Jalandhar to form the Bharatiya Jana Sangh in those areas.[22] And representatives from Madhya Bharat and Bhopal met at Indore on 2 December.[23] A convention took place in New Delhi on 21 October 1951 to lay the foundation of the new all-India party called the Bharatiya Jana Sangh.[24] The party from the very earliest tried to project for itself a non-communal, forward-looking and progressive image. This was tried to be done by two things: by opening its membership to all citizens of India irrespective of their caste which distinguished it from the Ram Rajya Parishad which refused membership to the Harijans, creed or religion—which distinguished it from the Hindu Mahasabha which refused membership to the non-Hindus. Secondly, the new party was to work for the Bharatiya Rashtra, and not for the Hindu Rashtra which was the aim of the Hindu Mahasabha. The new party stood for reconstruction of the Indian polity on the basis of 'Bharatiya Sanskriti' and 'Maryada' not for the Hindu religion. And furthermore, the party stood for social justice and the rule of law and democracy. It was to be staunchly nationalistic, determined to secure for India a position of honour and strength and due to it in view of it's of ancient culture, size and potential resources.

The party welcomed Muslims in its fold although it was opposed to the "suicidal policy of appeasement of Muslims,"[25] and called instead for 'Akhand Bharat' or the Union of India and Pakistan by 'peaceful means'.[26]

The relations of the Bharatiya Jana Sangh with the RSS have been a matter of controversy. The contribution of RSS workers in the formation of the Jana Sangh is not denied. As Jagdish Prasad Mathur, Secretary, All India Jana Sangh, wrote, "In bringing the Jana Sangh into being, Dr Mukherjee had received the co-operation of like-minded workers in the Rashtriya Swayamsevak Sangh."[27] But the Jana Sangh leader strongly refute the allegation that the Jana Sangh and the RSS are one, or that the former is just a political wing of the latter.[28] Dr Mukherjee tried to refute this allegation by pointing out that while some RSS workers joined the Jana Sangh, many Jana Sangh workers leader had no RSS connections.[29] This argument was reinforced by an official declaration from Golwalkar, the RSS Chief, in October 1951, to the effect that the RSS were free to cast their vote as they pleased.[30] The RSS, moreover, have always insisted that those who hold office in one organization should not hold office in another.

The question of relations between the Jana Sangh and the RSS became very controversial after the death of Dr Syama Prasad Mukherjee and it brought about a disrupt in the party. While some leaders of the Jana Sangh were eager to take in non RSS people, "a substantial section of RSS felt that there was little scope for non-RSS people who lacked the discipline which they shared; they believe that in the final analysis Jana Sangh depended upon the work and contribution of RSS members.[31] In 1954, reports appeared in the press of serious differences among the RSS and non-RSS members of the Jana Sangh, the latter alleging that the former was trying to gain complete control of the Jana Sangh. As a result of this dispute, Pandit Mauli Chandra Sharma, President of the Jana Sangh, after the death of Dr Mukherjee, resigned. Pandit Sharma was a great orator and a leading figure in the movement of the Hindi Sahitya Sammelan. While tendering his resignation, he publicly alleged that the RSS was trying to dominate the organization and policies of the Jana Sangh.

After the Fourth General Election, reports again appeared in a section of the press about the simmering differences in the Jana Sangh on the question of relations with the RSS,[32] and Balraj Madhok was spotted as the leader of the move to make the Jana Sangh completely independent of the RSS, when interviewed about his party's contacts with the RSS, Madhok said it had nothing to do with the formulation and implementation of the programme and policies of the Jana Sangh. Himself a Swayamsevak of RSS and its former organizer, he said that the Jana Sangh recognizes and respects the RSS, but the latter had no control as such over the former. But, at the same time, he did not rule out the possibility of some powerful RSS bosses trying to again control of the Jana Sangh. The RSS leaders deny any attempt on their part to dominate the affairs of the Jana Sangh. But at the same time, they assert that their aim is to dominate every aspect of national life with the ideology of the RSS.[33] As Golwalkar said, "the Sangh has accepted it as its duty to infuse every sector of national activity with a spirit of ardent and selfless patriotism, personal and national. In this sense, the Sangh (RSS) does seek to invade and 'dominate' every sphere of national life."[34] It is to be noted that the *Organiser* and the *Panchajanya* the non-official RSS weeklies, also act the non-official mouthpieces of the Jana Sangh. It cannot be denied that because of the large number of overlapping membership of both the RSS and Jana Sangh and also ideological affinity to some extent, both these organization view each other with sympathy and their members tend to closely co-operate, if not their office-bearers. On being asked by a correspondent as to whether Jana Sangh's assertion in its manifesto that it stood for a non-communal state did not conflict with the ideology of the RSS, which either controlled the party or wielded considerable influence over it, Atal Bihari Vajpayee, President of the Jana Sangh, replied that it vowed that either the party was not controlled by the RSS or that latter had changed its ideology. He further said, "Our stand is very clear. We are opposed to any discrimination or any favouritism."[35] It has to be pointed out here that at no time was there any formal, legal or constitutional arrangement between the two bodies, and in that sense it is quite correct to say that both these organizations are not one. But ideologically both these organizations exhort their members to be proud of their ancient (Hindus) heritage and fight against the inroads of the "decadent aspect of Western civilization."[36] A matter of vital difference between the two organizations, however, is the fact that while the membership of the Jana Sangh is open to all the Indian citizens, only the Hindus can become members of the RSS. In spite of this difference between the two parties, in practice the Jana Sangh is known to have tried to win votes on many occasions by calling on Hindu unity.[37] However, that makes the two organizations superficially look like the Siamese twins in the role of the organizing secretaries in the Jana Sangh. A former leader of the Jana Sangh revealed to the author that the organizing secretaries of the Jana Sangh are mostly people who are deputed by the RSS, who belong to the RSS cadre, and who can be withdrawn any moment by the RSS. The organizing secretaries play a vital role in the worker of organizing and expending the activities of the Jana Sangh. As the organizing secretaries belong to the regular RSS cadre, the possibility of the RSS wielding considerable influence in the Jana Sangh cannot be theoretically ruled out completely.

The Fourth General Elections created a new situation in India. For the first time the exponents of "cultural nationalism" with an air of superiority emerged on the political scene of India as a serious challenge not only to the Leftists or the Centrists but to all those Western-oriented dabblers in sophistication who had taken on them the responsibility to desperately rule over India's unsophisticated lot.

The Jana Sangh is the party that flourished fabulously, of course, mainly in Hindu-speaking areas, but also, simultaneously endeavoured to expand in the strongholds of its other active opponent with the active co-operation of the RSS. The world called it the expansion of Right wing extremism, reduced by materialistic Marxism and rejected by Anglo-Saxon pragmatism, gave birth of Jana Sangh into a political force to be reckoned with for quite a long time.

As the fourth General Election approached, the Jana Sangh after properly oiling its machinery threw into the battle of the ballot box 1567 contestants for Assembly sets, and fielded 242 candidates in the Parliamentary constituencies. Both the PSP and SSP could hardly contest 1547, Assembly seats and 230 Parliament seats. The two factions of the Communists participated in the elections with 1157 Assembly candidates and only 162 candidates for the Lok Sabha.

The mere weight and the massive man power that Jana Sangh could wield did not produce staggering results but none the less, they were beyond the expectations of politicians. No one predicted on the eve of the elections that Jana Sangh would bag 35 Parliamentary seats and 264 Assembly seats. The organizational structure and the soil of the RSS Cadre after all paid its organizational structure and the soil of the RSS Cadre after all paid its dividends. The percentage of votes polled in favour of Jana Sangh was 8.95 and 8.95 for the parliament and the Assembly respectively and they topped the list of all Opposition parties. Jana Sangh became the largest single party next to Congress in UP and Madhya Pradesh. It beat the

Congress in Delhi. The doubts about the Bharatiya Jana Sangh's reaching the maturity of a national political party were positively dispelled after the Fourth General Election and since than the history of Indian politics is being rewritten.

Since the Fourth General Election, the Jana Sangh like any other political party, under the public pressure, entered into the coalition governments with its deadly enemies, the Leftists. Then Jana Sangh took into its fold or at least invited men of other faiths and beliefs. Considering it the "Compulsion of the situation destroys its manoeuvrability by allowing China to rise between itself and other political parties."

The politics of united front in the north was in consonance with the slogan of "democracy, nationalism and realism" given by Balraj Madhok in his presidential address at the 13th annual session of the party held at Jalandhar, Punjab, on 30 April 1966.

Merger Proposals

Soon after the First General Elections of 1952, Dr Syama Prasad Mukherjee invited several Parliamentary parties to a conference in New Delhi to consider formation of a united front in the Parliament.[38] As a result of this conference, the United Democratic Party was formed in Parliament in June 1952. It consisted of thirty members of Parliament drawn from the Jana Sangh, the Hindu Mahasabha, the Tamil Nadu Toilers Party, Akali Dal, Gantantra Parishad and several independents. Dr Mukherjee was elected its leader. His great parliamentary skill enhanced his status, particularly his wordy duels with Pandit Nehru in the Lok Sabha. He felt that the massive victory of the Congress at the hustings was more due to the "existence of far too many candidates and small parties." Therefore, he exhorted that "the opposition parties should not filter away their energies but consolidate their position by presenting a united front based on a common programme dealing with urgent and vital problems. This was especially necessary inside the legislature so that due pressure might be brought to bear upon the ruling party and efficiency and purity of administration secured."[39] Due to programmatic similarity, particularly their joint campaign against the cow-slaughter, of Jammu and Kashmir for fuller integration of the State with the Indian Union, the three parties, the Jana Sangh, the Hindu Mahasabha and the Ram Rajya Parishad, came closer to each other and sentiments in favour of the merger of the three parties were expressed. But some Hindu Mahasabha leaders feared that in the event of merger, the Jana Sangh leadership would absorb the Mahasabha.[40] When the Praja Parishad agitation was at its peak Dr Syama Prasad Mukherjee died in mysterious circumstances in jail at Srinagar. NC Chatterjee tried to pursue the merger idea but the attempt failed due to three reasons. First, some Mahasabha leaders feared that their organization would be completely lost in the united party to be created after the merger.[41] Secondly, the Ram Rajya Parishad was not willing to sacrifice its 'Principles' in respects of religion which meant prohibition to the Harijans to become members of the new party. The Mahasabha also was not reconciled for admitting non-Hindus to the new party, and this was the view of VD Savarkar also that Parishad leaders to be obscurantist and outmoded in their outlook, ant at best to be only armchair politicians. Jana Sangh was not prepared to lose its identity, rather its idea was that these two parties should accept Sangh's Policies and merge with it. The membership of the party was, of course, to remain open for all Indian citizens.[42] Thus, there were many obstacles as well unwillingness on the part of leadership of the three parties for a merger. Foreign observer remarks, "Given all these obstacles and unwillingness of the leadership and of the rank and file of either organization to merger, one wonders not so much why the merger attempt failed as why it was attempted at all." Anyway, the merger attempt failed.

After the Fourth General Election, and particularly after the mid-term polls in Uttar Pradesh, attempt was initiated by Charan Singh, President of the Bharatiya Kranti Dal, for the creation of a new party by merger of the Jana Sangh, Bharatiya Kranti Dal, Swatantra Party and some other parties. This attempt also met its end. The *Organiser* wrote that while the Swatantra was a party of Seths and Sahukars, the Jana Sangh was a party of Babus and Banias and the middle-class people who are attracted to its slogan of nationalism, whereas the Kranti Dal had a single-point programme of making Charan Singh Chief Minister. Under such circumstances, the merger could not have succeeded unless these parties learnt to adjust themselves with each other by working together on certain common programmes. In fact, Vajpayee, the President of the Jana Sangh wanted such co-operation as a condition precedent for any sincere attempt at merger whereas Charan Singh wanted prior agreement on principles, programmes and ideology. Talks were abruptly terminated by the Bharatiya Kranti Dal because Charan Singh took absence of Vajpayee in the talks—Balraj Madhok represented for him in the talks as calculated to cause personal affront to him (Charan Singh).

There was a great split in the Congress in 1969, which started a trend of the disintegration of the Congress. However, there was dissolution of the Lok Sabha on 27 December 1970. In the wake of the adverse decisions of the Supreme Court in the bank Nationalization case in 1970. This paved the way for the Fifth General Election to the Lok Sabha.

The Jana Sangh contested 154 seats, but could win only 22 seats, retaining only old seats. The party lost 23 old seats while it gained 12 new seats. In the old house the party had 35 seats. This precipitous fall of the Jana Sangh in the Lok

Sabha was reflected in the elections for state Assemblies also in 1972.

In Bihar State Assembly the party had 34 members, which was reduced to 26 in 1972 Assembly election. In UP State Assembly the Jana Sangh had 98 seats after 1967 election which was reduced to 49 in 1969. Thus the party was showing a declining trend in the various elections.

The country experienced what came to be known as Indira wave in 1970, which was converged into the Indira tempest after India's victory over Pakistan on the Bangladesh issue. As the commentator remarked, the Indira wave "turned out to be a cyclone sweeping away almost all opposition parties to oblivion from where many of them will find it extremely hard to emerge."[43]

After the termination of the negotiation between the Jana Sangh and Bharatiya Kranti Dal by Charan Singh, seven parties and groups merged to Bharatiya Lok Dal on 29 August 1974. The emerging groups were the Swatantra Party, Bharatiya Kranti Dal, Utkal Congress, Samyukta Socialist Party faction of the former Samyukta Socialist Party, the Kisan Mazdoor Party and the Punjab Khetibari Zamindari Union. It hoped to develop itself as a national alternative to the Congress.

In the meanwhile, political events were taking place in Gujarat and Bihar, which turned out to be of great importance. There was a powerful movement of students and youths in Gujarat as a result of which the Congress ministry led by Chimanbhai Patel was dismissed in early 1974. In May 1975 Morarji Desai undertook a fast unto death demanding early elections for the State Assembly in Gujarat. The election to the Gujarat Assembly was held in early June 1975 where the Congress got only 75 seats and the Janata Front consisting of Congress (Organization), Jana Sangh, Bharatiya Lok Dal, Socialist and the few others, got 86 seats.

The share of the Jana Sangh was 18 seats.

The victory of Janata Front in Gujarat election marked a turning point in Indian party politics. A powerful movement spearheaded by students and youths under the guidance of Jayaprakash Narayan started for eradication of corruption and dissolution of Bihar State Legislative Assembly.

This resulted into proclamation of the State of National Emergency on 26 June 1975, banning of RSS and some other organizations and arrest of non-CPI opposition leaders.

The opposition leaders were released from jail a few months before the Sixth General Election for Lok Sabha held in March 1977. The Jana Sangh had been the danger of remaining alone. The RSS was banned and there was a demand for the ban on Jana Sangh also by some elements in the Congress. Therefore, the Jana Sangh agreed to merge with a new party consisting of the Bharatiya Lok Dal, the Congress (Organization) and the Socialist Party and fight the Lok Sabha election under the flag of an improvised party called the Janata Party. The unity of the non-CPI opposition parties under one flag provided a viable alternative to the Congress and the people in North India voted overwhelmingly for the Janata Party. There was a crippling defeat for the Congress and the Jana Sangh emerged as the largest constituent of the Janata Party in the Lok Sabha with about 96 seats. The outgoing Congress government saw the writing on the wall and revolved its ban on RSS and others organizations.

Janata Party formed government at the Centre under the leadership of Morarji Desai and Atal Bihari Vajpayee, a former Jana Sangh leader, was made External Affairs Minister of India.

The party now tested the fruit of unity with other party and it readily decided to merge its identity in the Janata Party. Thus, the Pratinidhi Sabha of the Bharatiya Jana Sangh meeting of New Delhi in April 1977 passed resolution merging its identity completely with the Janata Party. Satyendra Narayan Sinha, MP and President of Bihar State Janata Party, told the Jana Sangh delegates that they were leaving a 'Chhota Pariwar' (small family) to become a part of a large community.[44]

Thus Jana Sangh lost its separate identity but the RSS refused to merge with this new party, in spite of insistence by Janata Party President Chandra Shekhar to do so.[45] It has also been alleged by no less a person than Jagjivan Ram that all constituent parties of the Janata Party have retained their separate identity even after there formal merger with the Janata Party except the Congress for Democracy. It has been alleged by Indira Gandhi and several other leaders of the Congress(I) that the Jana Sangh was dominating the Janata Party and a time is not far when the Jana Sangh will completely devour the Janata Party. It was alleged that the front organizations of the Jana Sangh like the Akhil Bharatiya Vidyarthi Parishad and Bharatiya Mazdoor Sangh and Bharatiya Mahila Sangh, etc have refused to merge with the Janata Party. The critics cite the example of Nanaji Deshmukh, the former Organizing Secretary of the Bharatiya Jana Sangh who preferred the non-glamourous but strategic post of General Secretaryship of Janata Party to a Cabinet Ministership in the Union Government. The critics also cite the devious role of the Jana Sangh in dividing the posts of Chief Ministers of 8 north Indian States between itself and the former Bharatiya Lok Dal on a fifty-fifty ratio after the June 1977 State Assembly elections capturing Madhya Pradesh, Rajasthan, Himachal Pradesh and Delhi. The Janata Party Working Committee had earlier decided to give free hand to the State Janata Legislative Parties without any muddling from the Central leadership. This was an occasion for shedding old colours by the erstwhile constituents of the Janata Party and facilitating the way for complete integration, which the critics allege, will lead to the disintegration of the Janata Party and its eventual domination by the Jana Sangh. The critics say that Jana Sangh has not merged, it has merely put its signboard beneath the carpet for a temporary period for purely strategic reasons and the time is not far when it will discard its Janata garb and will emerge with this added strength. The present investigation is inclined to agree with this view, and therefore, the author has used an expression as if the Jana Sangh is alive.

In the Third General Election which was held in 1962, the Congress won 361 seats (out of 494) while the position of the Opposition was poor. It was the CPI only which secured maximum 29 seats. Swatantra party got 22 and BJS secured 14, PSP got 12, SP under Lohiya 6, Hindu Mahasabha 1, Muslim League 2 and Akali Dal 3.

With the elections of 1967 the Indian political system entered into a new phase. The overwhelming majority of the Congress was reduced to 284 seats (out of 520) in the Lok Sabha which was sufficient to form the government. In many state legislature opposition parties were able to force the Congress out of office. According to political observers, this change in the Indian Political system took place due to departure of Pandit Nehru. The Congress had fought the first three elections under the dominating influence of Nehru. But in May 1964 India lost Nehru and Congress its undisputed leader. The loss of confidence of the nation in Nehru shocked the Congress. Analysis of the development of opposition Parties in India during Nehru regime reveals the fact that no opposition leader would successfully compete with Nehru. No doubt Dr Lohiya, Asok Mehta, and others had established their reputation in the country but they failed to organize a strong opposition.[46] The Communist Party had been consistently working and trying hard to achieve the power but they failed. Because their methods were not liked by the people.[47]

The Jana Sangh since its inception had been trying hard to achieve the power but it could not get progress because of its association with RSS which was responsible for the murder of Mahatma Gandhi.

After the demise of Pandit Nehru, the Opposition began to expect too much and got involved into political activities with full strength. That is why their position improved in the States in the elections of 1967. The opposition leaders began to criticise the failure of the Congress policies and incapacity of its leaders. Several States had gone out of the Congress hands. In Bihar, UP, West Bengal, Kerala, Madras, Tripura etc, the opposition party had turned into ruling party.

In 1967 the opposition had been speaking in hope and ambitiously of offering an all out fight to the Congress. But they failed to form a strong opposition and they fought elections without any alliance. That is why, the Congress once again remained in power in the Centre. However the majority of the Congress reduced in the Centre. It secured 284 seats while 236 seats went to the opposition. The Swatantra Party, and Jana Sangh, CPI, CPI(M), SSP, PSP, DMK, ADMK, all improved their position.[48]

A detailed study of Congress declination shows that the Congress had moved towards deterioration. It all happened due to the failure of Congress on the economic front, in spite of its declared policy of socialistic pattern of society. The Congress had failed to reduce the gap between the rich and the poor. The massive swing against the Congress in the states was due to social unrest and economic discontent among large section of population.[49] It provided suitable chance for the opposition parties to improve their position. The opposition parties moved towards the politics of coalition. On the other hand differences took place among the leaders of the Congress. In the past, Congress had failed to achieve its goals. The Right wing leaders of the Congress were the main obstacles on the progressive path of the Congress. The Congress had moved towards the path of disunity and division. The Left wing leaders under the leadership of Indira Gandhi were not ready to make any compromise with the Right wing leaders. Indira Gandhi had fully realized that the reason of downfall of Congress at the Centre and in States was party's reluctance and negligence to give practical shape of the socialistic pattern of society. In the words of Chandrika Singh,

> "her observation of the changing political attitude of the Indian electorate and rising strength of the leftist forces and analysis of her own party's traditional attitude convinced Indira Gandhi that the popularity of the Congress could not be achieved unless a basic change was made in its way of working and thinking."[50]

Indira Gandhi despite the heavy protest from the Right wing of the Congress advised the President to issue an Ordinance for nationalization of the major 14 commercial banks.[51]

This step of Indira Gandhi unpleased her opponents inside the party. As a result, a fight appeared in the Congress which ultimately resulted in the split of the Congress party. This provided an ample opportunity for the opposition parties to weaken the strength of the Congress.

In the Lok Sabha Elections of 1971 the Opposition leaders began to expect victory. In fact, in was a very sensational election in comparison to all other parliamentary elections. Despite multi-political party system there was tough and direct fight between the Leftist and the Rightist forces of the country. The basic issue before the electorate was to choose either

Indira Gandhi's brand of socialism or the status quo supported by the reactionary forces.

All the opposition parties were applying hard efforts to dislodge the Congress from the politics. But they could not organize themselves which enabled Congress to win the mid-term election of 1971.

Almost every party of the left and right of the Congress was affected to a greater or lesser extent by the break of Congress Party.

Commenting on the Lok Sabha elections of 1971 Hartaman said that for the first time since independence there was no longer any real national party contesting all or nearly all seats. Neither faction of the Congress had in this respect filled the void left by the split in that party. Congress(I) contested 442 seats while the Democratic Front adopted 450 agreed candidates.[52]

For the first time two alliances were fighting each other. In the words of Nijalingappa,

> "there are in fact two coalitions today, one is veiled coalition of the ruling party with the Communist within and without, the Muslim League and the DM, and the other is an open front between any national and democratic parties, mainly the Congress, the Swatantra, the Jana Sangh and the SSP. The BHD and the PSP have joined this in many places."[53]

Result of the 1971 elections proved that Indira Gandhi was still the most popular leader of the country. This result also proved that the Congress(I) was the genuine political party of the country. Out of 442 contested seats, Congress(I) secured 350 seats while its splinter group known as Congress(O) hardly got 16 seats. CPI(M) emerged as the largest opposition group of the Lok Sabha securing 25 seats. The position of other opposition parties remained poor. Indira Gandhi believed that the victory in 1971 elections was unique. One of the causes of her thumping victory was her solving the Bangladesh problem, bifurcating Pakistan into two political and independent parts.

Indira Gandhi as Prime Minister gave a new dynamic direction to the Indian politics as well as international politics. She adopted several schemes to gear up the economic front of the country. In fact the election of 1971 had made Indira Gandhi as the champion of the causes of the Leftist political forces. Her policies and her schemes raised new hopes and aspirations among the people of the down-trodden section of the people. To check the power of judiciary, she began to curtail the power of the Supreme Court and High Courts, vide passing the constitutional amendment acts. A tussle between the Parliament and judiciary had been observed. The judiciary was putting obstacles on the progressive path of the Congress laid by Indira Gandhi. Her steps like nationalization of commercial banks, and abolition of privy purses had been challenged in the Supreme Court. Therefore, she brought 24th and 25th constitutional amendment acts which curtailed the powers of judicial review by the Indian judiciary.[54]

The steps of Indira Gandhi altered the leaders of the opposition parties who were still traditional in their approach. They began to blame Indira Gandhi and block her path in the Parliament. There were tough debates in the Parliament but, Indira Gandhi was not going to bow down. Jayaprakash Narayan became very much vocal against Indira Gandhi. He began to blame her as a dictator. He said that "this is a slippery path and will end up not in democratic socialism but in dictatorial communism."[55] In the words of Chandrika Singh,

> "It was Jayaprakash Narayan who gave lead to the people of Bihar in particular and other citizens of the country in

> general for bringing about total revolution with the results that all the educational institutions of Bihar transformed into deserts because the students took part in the JP's mass revolution by boycotting their classes and examinations. He did not hesitate to call upon the personnel of the armed forces to participate in his revolution."[56]

JP appeared as an undisputed leader among the opposition parties in India. Getting inspiration and inducement from him, all the opposition parties who were against the Congress(I), began to unite together with a view to finish up the mounting strength of Congress(I). Meanwhile the Allahabad High Court found Indira Gandhi "guilty of having committed corrupt practices under Section 123(7) of the Representation of the Peoples Act. She was debarred from the membership of Indian Parliament for a period of six year. But on the appeal of Indira Gandhi, Supreme Court allowed her to continue as Prime Minister and enjoy rights and privileges vested in the post until the final decision given.

The stay order of the Supreme Court caused a great political upheaval in the country. The opposition leaders under the leadership of Jayaprakash Narayan were not in mood to allow Indira Gandhi to remain in power. They began to demand quick resignation from her. To blame and harass Indira Gandhi they began to stage movements against her all over the country. Jayaprakash Narayan was not only vocal but also against Indira Gandhi. He took the lead of 'Indira Hatao Morcha'. By the last week of June 1975 the movement against Indira Gandhi took decisive path. It appeared that the country was going to pass through a stormy political phase. Citizens of the country had never witnessed such political activity in India after independence. The capital of the country was crowded with the people who had come from different corners of the country to join the demonstration and rallies.[57] There was a plan to gherao some ministers and enter the premises of Indira Gandhi's residence by breaking up the Section 144 of the IPC. There was also a plan to adopt the technique of mass movement of nationwide scale.

Indira Gandhi was more aware than her opponents. In her defence and in the defence of the country she promulgated emergency in the country on the ground of internal disturbance on 26 June 1975.[58] There upon she strongly tightened the machinery of the government and arrested a number of activist including the top political leaders of the country overnight. Even Jayaprakash Narayan was not spared. Her son Sanjay Gandhi became very much active on her behalf and became instrumental during the period of emergency. To keep a check on the judiciary she brought the 42nd Constitutional Amendment Act 1976 within the parliament. On the other hand she also took up several schemes to push up the economic progress of the country and maintain punctuality and discipline among the government officials and personals. In fact she became too hard, which caused much inconvenience to the people.

Criticism not too openly, but in a hidden way began to come. Murmuring and groaning against the rule of Indira Gandhi were coming in the air. But she did not care for it.

To prove herself as a true democratic leader Indira Gandhi liked to go for mandate in December 1976. So she decided to go for polls in March 1977. She was expecting absolute majority but her expectation could not be realized. When the elections were held and results were published, her surprise had no bound, because not only her party had been badly defeated but she had also been rejected from her own constituency.

The cause of the defeat of Indira Gandhi and her party was the excesses committed during emergency by her government.

Moreover, the opposition leaders such as Congress (Organization), Bharatiya Jana Sangh, Bharatiya Lok Dal, and Socialist Party merged together and formed a new political party known as the Janata Party with a view to defeat Indira Gandhi. It was for the first time in the history of India, that political parties which formed a strong opposition came in power. By forgetting their personal rivalries and even party's ideologies they formed a single political party. After the election, Morarji Desai was chosen as the leader of the party, who became the Prime Minister. The Janata Party got majority not only with centre but in the Northern States also like Bihar, Uttar Pradesh, Haryana, Madhya Pradesh etc.

The Janata Party could not remain in power for a longer period because dissension took place among the Janata leaders for powers and principles. In fact, the merger was not only principle but on circumstances. They had merged together for power not for principles. Therefore, they began to quarrel among themselves, soon after formation of the Janata Party government. Moreover in spite of doing some constructive works for the progress and prosperity for the people and the country, they began to retaliate against Indira Gandhi and her colleagues. The rivalry for power among the Janata leaders for the Prime Ministership came at climax by mid-1979. Chaudhary Charan Singh and Jagjivan Ram began to take interest for becoming the Prime Minister. Though, Jayaprakash Narayan tried from his sick-bed, to bring unity among the Janata leaders but all in vain. Charan Singh became totally against Morarji Desai and withdrew his support. He was assured by Indira Gandhi of her party's support in the Parliament. With the help of Indira Gandhi the dream of Charan Singh was fulfilled and he became the Prime Minister of India. But surprisingly enough she withdrew her support to Charan Singh as a result his government became a minority. The then

President Neelam Sanjiva Reddy had to prove the majority to the claimants of majority party. Before the majority would have been proved, Charan Singh suggested the President to go for mid-term polls by dissolving the Lok Sabha.[59]

The country once again went to polls on January 2 and 4, 1980. This time the observers witnessed a total change in the political and voting behaviour in the country. Chandrika Singh rightly remarked that

> "the shadow of castism which is the permanent feature of the Indian voting behaviour was thrown of and the basic motivation behind the electorate was 'Indira Bulao'. As a result the Congress(I) once more appeared on the political scene with thumping victory despite of number of charges levelled against its leaders by the Janata government. In this very 'Indira Bulao' wave all other political parties except BJP and the Lok Dal were badly swept away."[60]

Thus, Indira Gandhi once again became the popular leader of the country while the opposition parties not only lost power but also lost position. Indira Gandhi began to take deep interest in the national and international politics. She appeared as an international leader and became the Chairman of Non-Aligned Movement in March 1983. Meanwhile the extremist politics of Punjab with the support of foreign powers became intolerable. On the other hand, Indira Gandhi was determined to defend the national integrity. So with a view to teach the extremists a lesson and to defend the territorial integrity she implemented the Blue Star Operation in Punjab on 2 June 1984.[61] During the operation the leader of Punjabi extremists, Bhindranwala was killed along with several extremists. This caused unrest among the Sikhs of Punjab. To retaliate, the extremists succeeded in murdering Indira Gandhi in her own residence on 31 October 1984.[62]

The murder of Indira Gandhi was the greatest loss to India. It caused unrest in the country and bloodshed. In the communal riots many Sikhs were killed and their property was looted. Meanwhile Rajiv Gandhi, the eldest son of Indira Gandhi, was sworn as the Prime Minister of the country. He soon after taking the lead, established peace by controlling the situation.

Rajiv Gandhi and his party had achieved reputation even within a short period. Hence, in the parliamentary elections of 1985 his party got absolute majority. He was appointed as the Prime Minister of India. It was believed that the murder of Indira Gandhi had created a great deal of sympathy for Rajiv Gandhi.

Rajiv Gandhi soon declared that he would abide by the principles of Mahatma Gandhi, Pandit Jawaharlal Nehru and Indira Gandhi. He solved some vital issues of the country such as the problem of Assam, Mizoram and Punjab by having alliances with the dissident leaders. The centenary of the Congress also took place during the regime of Rajiv Gandhi. He took much interest in it and made several promises to develop India and her people. Rajiv Gandhi, though new in politics, had by now established reputation in the international field.

To stop the politics of defection he brought the Anti-Defection Bill in the Parliament and got it passed. Later, he was busy with the Tamil problems in Sri Lanka, where he showed much courage and wisdom by signing Peace Accord with the Government of Sri Lanka on 29 July 1987, and deployed Indian Peace Keeping Force in Sri Lanka.

Thus, it is clear that the party politics of India which took dynamic shape after independence is much interesting. No doubt, India still lacked strong opposition party, but the Indian political behaviour developed. The Congress was still having dominance over power, but a new consciousness among the opposition leaders is coming up. The opposition leaders levelled charges of corruption against the government of Rajiv Gandhi. His closest supporter like, Vishwanath Pratap Singh deserted him along with other leaders such as VC Shukla. The opposition was trying to unite together. The Congress lost power in several states; West Bengal, Kerala, Madras, Andhra Pradesh, Karnataka were out of the Congress's hands. It also lost its position in Haryana and Punjab during recent legislative assemblies. It appeared that the position of the Congress was weakening. The opposition leaders were demanding mid-term elections in the centre. But Rajiv Gandhi was not ready to face the electorate before the completion of his tenure. But how long the Congress could have avoided the elections? The tenure of the Parliament was going to be over in 1989. The coming parliamentary elections could only prove what change will take in the political activities of the country.

References

1. Jagdish Prasad Mathur: "A Historical Glance at Jana Sangh"; *The Sunday Searchlight* (Patna: 28 December 1969, p 1).
2. DR Goyal: "The Jana Sangh Party", *Weekly Round Table* (New Delhi: Vol 1, No 50, January 15, 1973, p 7).
3. JA Curan, Jr, *Militant Hinduism in India: A Study of the RSS* (New York: Institute of Pacific Relations, 1951, p 13). The RSS according to its constitution is a 'cultural' organization. According to a foreign observer, "It is a tightly knit, disciplined, hierarchical organization seeking to incorporate larger and larger segments of the Public within its ranks. Its primary aim is to establish with its own groups a model of a revitalized Hindu society and eventually to secure.
4. VP Varma: *Modern Indian Political Thought* (Agra, Lakshmi Narayan Agarwal, 1964), p 396.
5. MS Golwalkar: *Why Hindu Rashtra* (Bangalore, Rashtriya Swayamsevak Sangh), p 21.

6. MS Golwalkar: *Not Socialism but Hindu Rashtra* (Bangalore, RSS, 1964), p 31.
7. Syama Prasad Mukherjee: *Why Bharatiya Jana Sangh* (A Booklet published by Bharatiya Jana Sangh), p 3.
8. *Principles and Policy*, *op cit*, p 14.
9. VP Varma: *op cit*, pp 359-60.
10. *Ibid*.
11. *Principles and Policy*, *op cit*, p 9.
12. DP Ghosh: Presidential Address at the Fifth Annual Session Bharatiya Jana Sangh at New Delhi, December 1950.
13. Myron Weiner: *Party Politic in India: The Development of a Multi-Party System* (Princeton, Princeton University Press, 1975), p 184.
14. *Ibid*.
15. *Ibid*, p 185.
16. Balraj Madhok: *Dr Syama Prasad Mukherjee: A Biography* (New Delhi, Deepak Prakashan, 1954), p 45.
17. Jagdish Prasad Mathur: *op cit*.
18. VR Oak: Quoted by Weiner, *op cit*, p 186.
19. Shankar Joshi: "Speech at Karnavati", 10 November 1949, quoted by Curran, *op cit*, p 27.
20. *The Hindu* (Madras), 8 January 1951.
21. See the *Organiser*, 7 May 1951.
22. *Organiser*, 11 June 1951.
23. Jagdish Prasad, Mathur, *op cit*.
24. *Hindustan Times* (New Delhi), 22 October 1951; *Organiser*, 29 October 1951.
25. 'Why Bharatiya Jana Sangh': The Presidential Address of Dr Syama Prasad Mukherjee at the opening Convention of Akhil Bharatiya Jana Sangh (Delhi, Bharat Mudranalaya, 1951), p 4.
26. Dr Mukherjee in his presidential address declared: "Partition of Bharat was a tragic folly. We believe in the goal of a reunited Bharat through peaceful means. So long as Pakistan continues we will urge a policy of strict reciprocity." *Ibid*, pp 6-7.
27. Jagdish Prasad, Mathur, *op cit*.

28. Welles Hangen wrote: "The sinister side of the Jana Sangh is its undercover association with the Rashtriya Swayamsevak Sangh (RSS) or National Volunteer Association, the militant Hindu organization one of whose members assassinated Gandhi," *After Nehru, Who?*, p 19.
29. *Organiser*, 29 October 1951.
30. *Ibid*.
31. Weiner, *op cit*, p 198. Weiner thinks that it "was this lack of reliance upon non-RSS members and leaders which enabled the party to survive and grow even after the death of Syama Prasad Mukherjee in 1953. *Ibid*.
32. See report in *Statesman*, 2 November 1954 and other papers of this period.
33. See the *Link Weekly* and *Mainstream Weekly* of 1968, particularly of the latter half of the year.
34. Madhav Sadashiv Golwalkar: "Yes RSS Does Want to Dominate Every Walk of National Life", *Organiser*, 2 November 1964, pp 9-10.
35. See *The Searchlight* (Patna, Vol XXI, No 24, 25 January 1971), p 1. Column 1-2 UXI News mesage headlined, "Front Reaches Agreement on 450 Seats".
36. See Golwalkar Speech at the "Vishva Hindu Parishad Meet", *The Searchlight*, 29 January 1971, p 7
37. Donald E. Smith: *India, as a Secular State* (Princeton, Princeton University Press, 1963), pp 469-479.
38. *Organiser*, 16 March 1952, p 1.
39. *Organiser* 12 May 1952, p 8.
40. Ashutosh Lahiri: "Immediate Problems before the Mahasabha", *Hindu Outlook*, 3 May 1953, p 2.
41. Indra Prakash: "Liquidation under the Grab of a United Front", *Hindu Outlook*, 30 August 1953, p 3.
42. Mauli Chandra Sharma's speech at Agra on 26 August 1953, *Hindustan Times*, 27 August 1953.
43. Inder Malhotra: "Indira Wields the Broom", *The Illustrated Weekly of India* (Bombay), 29 March 1972.

44. "Jana Sangh Endorses Merger Decision", *The Sunday Standard*, 1 May 1977, p 6.
45. "RSS View of India Ten Years Hence", *Organiser,* Vol XXIX, No I, 28 May 1977.
46. S Harrison, "India the Most Dangerous Decades", p 293.
47. Welles Hangen, *After Nehru, Who?*, New York, 1963, p 184.
48. For detailed study, See the *Parliamentary Elections,* 1967.
49. Monthly Public Opinion Survey of the Indian Institute of Public Opinion, New Delhi, November 1966, pp 6-7.
50. Chandrika Singh, *Communist and Socialist movement in India*, *op cit*, p 158.
51. *Times of India*, New Delhi July 20, 1970.
52. Hartmann, *Political Parties in India, op cit*, p 232.
53. *Hindustan Times*, New Delhi, 11.2.1971.
54. For detailed study of 24 and 25 Constitutional Amendment Acts, see DD Basu's, *Constitutional Law of India*, New Delhi, 1977, pp 2, 121, 122, 140 and 438.
55. Quoted in Kuldip Nayar's *Suppression of Judges*, New Delhi, 1973, pp 71-77.
56. Chandrika Singh, *Communist and Socialist Movement in India*, *op cit*, p 162.
57. *The Indian Express*, New Delhi, June and 26, 1975
58. *Why Emergency?,* A booklet issued from the Ministry of Home Affairs, New Delhi, 1975.
59. Hartmann, *Political Parties in India*, *op cit*, p 251.
60. Chandrika Singh, *Communist and Socialist Movement in India*, *op cit*, p 168.
61. *The Indian Express*, New Delhi, 3 June 1984.
62. *The Times of India*, New Delhi, 1 November 1984.

CHAPTER 3

Principles and Ideology

The Jana Sangh is a political party with certain ideologies. Except the Jana Sangh probably, there is no other non-Communist parties in India that plays the role similar to the programme and activities role as of Jana Sangh.

The objective of the Bharatiya Jana Sangh is to rebuild Bharat on the basis of 'Bharatiya Sanskriti' and 'Maryada' and as a political, social and economic democracy, guaranteeing equality of opportunity and liberty to all its citizens so as to build up a prosperous, powerful and united nation, which is progressive, modern and enlightened and is able to withstand the aggressive designs of others and to exert herself in the committee of nations for the establishment of world peace.[1] The Jana Sangh thinks that the nations have been drifting without any sense of direction and purpose and has been caught up in a cesspool of inertia and helplessness. This mood of cynicism and difference is not only unbecoming of a great nation like ours, it can be positively dangerous for its very existence.[2] The country must be pulled out of this morass immediately and the Jana Sangh wants to assume leadership in this direction. The Jana Sangh thinks that the "main reason for the present state of affairs is the failure of the leadership to comprehend the fundamental springs of national vitality, and their attempt to impose on the people alien to ideologies and life-values. In their impatience for economic progress, the leadership has been prone to ignore the nation's real 'self' and has adopted foreign pattern recklessly.[3] On the other hand,

Jana Sangh thinks that the 'Bharatiya Sanskriti' offers the right philosophical substratum on the basis of which national progress and world peace could be achieved. This is because, the "basic truths propounded by 'Bharatiya Sanskriti' have a validity beyond country and age," and they "will provide a direction not only for our own advancement, but for the world's progress as well."[4] Belief in the efficacy of the 'Bharatiya Sanskriti' to solve all the maladies affecting the nation and the world is basic to the ideology of the Jana Sangh. And the Jana Sangh wants to project itself as "the modern political expression of that national-self which has been trying to manifest itself after a period of bondage of a thousand years."[5]

The Jana Sangh does not want to impose India's will on the world. It rather believes that

> "the rise and fall of nations depends very much on how far their conduct has been in conformity with their own genius. But despite these variegated characteristics of their different nations can pay a complementary role in building up of world unity. If any nation does not do so and impairs unity it should be considered a perversity."[6]

The ideal of the Jana Sangh is to establish Dharma Rajya as the rule of law in India. The "Dharma Rajya ensures on the one hand a curb on arbitrariness and totalitarianism, and, on the other, it prevent democracy from degenerating into monocracy."[7] The Dharma Rajya will be a non-sectarian State and not a Theocracy. Its essential feature is "tolerance and respect for all faiths and creeds." Freedom of worship and conscience is guaranteed to all and the state, and does not discriminate against any one on the grounds of religion, either in the formulation of policy or in its implementation.[8]

The Jana Sangh has given the name 'Integral Humanism' to the sum total of various features of 'Bharatiya Sanskriti', and this ideal is sought to determine the direction of the party.[9] The Jana Sangh does not subscribe to socialism as such because it, in the eyes of the party, is "an incomplete and top-sided philosophy, grounded on mere materialistic values," whose acceptance as a creed might expose the country to the risks of statism. The party, however, has no quarrel with socialism's concern for the underdog or its insistence on social justice and equality.[10] According to Jana Sangh, the current controversy about public sector and private sector is "unreal and harmful to national interests." According to it,

> "what this country really needs today is a national sector in which private enterprise and resources of the state are coordinated and co-related in the interest of maximum, and more efficient, production."[11]

The idealism of the Jana Sangh does not mean any doctrinaire obtuseness, as the party claims, and the programme emanating from this idealism is sought to be grounded in realism and the conditions prevailing in India today. The Jana Sangh lays down the following policies and programmes:

One Country

According to the party, this entire Bharatvarsha has always been one and the unity and indivisibility of the country has been manifested in all fields—economic, political and social. In expression of their sacred and unflinching love for every particle of their land, the people have been worshipping it as *Bharat Mata*. From this follows the Jana Sangh's opposition to the existence of Pakistan which, in the eye of the party, represents "a refutation of the fact of one nationhood and one culture.[12] Therefore, it shall be an objective of Jana Sangh policies to end the separation of India and Pakistan and to bring the two together."[13] The re-establishment of 'Akhand Bharat' is the supreme aim of the party and for this the party "shall neither rest nor it shall wear in the pursuit of its efforts," said the Principal DP Ghosh in his presidential address at the Sixth Annual Session of the Jana Sangh in 1958.

One People

The party believes that all people living in this land of Bharat and "cherishing a filial attachment to it constitute one people."[14] Many diversities are apparent, which are an index actually of free growth and cultural plenitude, but beneath them unity has endured. The party will make efforts to strengthen this unity of the Indian people by fostering a feeling of equality and fraternity.

One Culture

The party stands for one culture in India. It concedes that in a vast country like India,

> "it was but natural that somewhat different patterns of life should have grown in different areas and sections. But all of them stand integrally united in 'Bharatiya Sanskriti' which has never been tied to the strings of any particular dogma or creed. The 'Bharatiya' culture is thus, like Bharatvarsha, one and indivisible. Any talk of composite culture, therefore, is not only untrue but also dangerous for it tends to weaken national unity and encourage fissiparous tendencies."[15]

One Nation

Jana Sangh defines a nation as a "society which has filial devotion to its own land and a characteristic genius of its own,"[16] and holds that India is an ancient nation. The dawn of independence in 1947, therefore, did not mark the birth of any new nation. It was only unfolding of a new chapter in its long history. In view of the party,

> "the basis of Indian nationalism is loyalty to the whole of Bharat and its eternal and distinctive culture."[17]

On the question of religious minorities, the party claims to hold a liberal view, and considers it "an essential feature of nationalism and democracy that minorities be treated with tolerance and without discrimination." The party guarantees such treatment to "all kinds of minorities," but it is opposed to religion getting mixed up with politics or demands being made for special privileges on grounds of religion."[18] The party thinks that in order to ensure the total loyalty of all citizens, "The government will have to make a conscious efforts to change the historical thought processes which have given birth to the Pakistani mentality."[19] At the 16th All-India session of the party held at Patna in December 1969, Vajpayee gave a call for 'Indianization' of the whole people to bring home the awareness of our nationhood to 'everyone', and particularly the Muslim community which "had come under the influence of Jinnah's two-nation theory."[20] Vajpayee defined 'Indianization' by saying that "the first and foremost loyalty of all citizens should be to India, irrespective of their differences in respect of religion, language, province and community."[21] Prof Balraj Madhok while explaining the meaning of the term Jana Sangh said that "only he can be called a 'Jana' of India, who looks upon Bharat as his own *Janani* (mother) and who owns its history, owns its past and owns it future."[22]

Political Structure

The Jana Sangh stands for a unitary form of government and is against the federal state because only the former "can effectively contribute to the invigoration of the one nationhood based on one country, one people and one culture" whereas the latter tends to hamper national integration.[23]

Foreign Policy

The Jana Sangh feels that the basis of a country's foreign policy should be the "protection of enlightened self-interest of the nation,"[24] and not of an inflexible dogma, like non-alignment. This calls for a "dynamic and strong" foreign policy, and it "would be unwise to adopt rigid postures,"[25] in the realm of foreign affairs. The party urges for a relaxation of the policy of non-alignment, which it regards as the very antithesis of foreign relations[26] and feels that assumption that the world is divided into two power-blocs and that we have to be either aligned with one of these, or non-aligned, is now outdated and irrelevant to the needs of the time.[27] The working committee of the Jana Sangh at Vijayawada in January 1965, criticized the Congress leaders for their obsession with platitudes like world-peace and co-existence and with cliches and catchwords like non-alignment which have little relevance in the new situation which has coloured our vision and stunned our sense of perception and capacity to adjust to these fast changing realities of the world situation. The party urges that the ultimate objectives of the nation must always be kept in view and that the assessment of friends and enemies in the world ought to be made on a realistic basis, and policies formulated with due regard to the circumstances.[28] Prof Balraj Madhok while speaking at Ahmedabad, said that so far as International relations are concerned, there is no place for charity, morality or justice in it. The only basis of foreign policy is and should be self-interest[29] of the nation. In support of his statement, Prof Madhok quoted the reply of Salisbury to Queen Victoria that "England has no permanent friends, England has no permanent enemies. She has only permanent interests."[30] Speaking in the Lok Sabha, Prof Madhok said, "the foreign policy of any country is not a question of platitudes; it is not a question of some dogmatism, it is not a question of some kind of idealistic policies, but it is a question of realism, it is a question of situations as they face us,"[31] and charged that Pandit Nehru's foreign policy had been a colossal failure as it was marked by ideological myopia—"to self-immolation arising from dogmatic belief that foreign policy is linked in a fatalistic way to economic ideology." Jana Sangh, however, is in full support to strengthen the United Nations as an instrument of world peace and cooperation but wants a permanent seat for India in the UN Security Council.[32] Believing that diversity is inherent in the world, as is propounded by the Indian philosophy, Jana Sangh recognizes the rights of every nation to evolve its way of life according to its own genius, and is opposed to imposing the same pattern on all nations.[33] The party holds that so long as imperialism and colonialism subsist in the world, so long as the tendency to look down on others because of their colour, creed or belief exists, so long as there are wide economic disparities between nation and nation and the consequent exploitation by some of others, so long as some two or three big nations hold themselves as the arbiters of peace or war in the world, there can be no relaxation in world tension and we will always be on the brink of a precipice. Therefore, it is necessary, in the view of the Jana Sangh, that subject nations are emancipated, human rights honoured everywhere, disparities among national standards reduced, the sphere of cooperation among them enlarged and as an international body, the United Nations Organization developed on a stronger, more representative, and just basis.[34] Similarly, the *Manifesto and Programme* of the Jana Sangh, 1958, spelt the party's view on world peace and allied problems. It said: "It is the confirmed view of the Jana Sangh that permanent peace is not possible so long as there exist political slavery, economic exploitation, social discrimination and selfish lust for power." As a party claiming to be wide awake to the reality of the world situation, Jana Sangh feels that in this competitive world, weakness is a curse and that if any nation wants to live freely and honourably it is essential to have military and economic strength commensurate with the size and potential of the country. Without strength, the urge for peace can encourage evil intentions (on the part of other nations) and so ultimately prove fatal for peace itself.[35] This is what has actually happened with India when it became a victim of aggression of Pakistan and Red China. Therefore, Jana Sangh called for the manufacture of atom bombs by India and the creation of a national nuclear deterrent at its Bhopal Convention in 1962.[35] Since, then it has carried a relentless campaign for this objective.

Attitude Towards Pakistan and Red China

In the view of Jana Sangh, "Both Communist China as well as Pakistan are India's natural enemies"[36] who have committed aggression on India and illegally seized large chunks of Indian territory and who operate in the international field to injure India whenever possible.

Jana Sangh holds that the people of Pakistan are basically part of the Indian nation and they have fallen prey to the motives of the separatist political forces.[37] Pakistan is going to remain India's "enemy so long as it exists."[38] Enmity towards India lies in the very genesis of Pakistan.[39] The party feels that the tension between India and Pakistan could be put to a stop, only through the achievement of 'Akhand Bharat'. But as long as Pakistan exists, India should strictly follow the policy of 'reciprocity', which means hitting back Pakistan whenever it says or does something harmful against India. Speaking in the Lok Sabha, Prof Balraj Madhok said that "Pakistan is an enemy and I do not agree with those people who think that by following a friendly policy we can be friend of Pakistan."[40] The party feels that policy of appeasement followed by India towards Pakistan has been the biggest prop to the anti-India stance of the rulers of Pakistan. If India were to adopt an attitude of firmness towards Pakistan, Pakistan's worked-up hostility towards India would not last long[41] and Pakistan's rulers will be forced to see the reason and behave accordingly. Jana Sangh in this way wants to be friendly with Pakistan but 'firmly' believes that appeasement is no way to friendship and goodwill[42] the party demands that Pakistan should cede to India adequate territory to re-settle the large number of Hindus driven out by force from East Pakistan.[43] Jana Sangh feels that the Kashmir question has become complicated because of the vacillating and "faltering" attitude of the Congress Party, and particularly of the late Pandit Nehru. The Manifesto of the Jana Sangh of 1962 said that the party looks upon any attack on Kashmir as an attack on India and will take all measures to liberate Indian territory illegally occupied by Pakistan and China. The 1967 Manifesto also reiterated the same stand. The Sangh pleads for the deletion of Article 370 from the Indian Constitution which accords special status to Kashmir as the Indian Union. The deletion of Article 370 will, according to the Sangh, give proof of the Government of India's firmness and the powers which want to create disturbance there, will cease to have the opportunity of exploiting the prevalent uncertainty. According to the Sangh, this article has betrayed the communal and unrealistic approach of the Government of India to this Vital issue and it (Article 370) has become the symbol of separatism for the separatist and communal elements in Kashmir.[44] Meeting of the Working Committee of Sangh at Patna on December 1964 held that abrogation of this article at one stroke could be the only patriotic and practical reply to Pakistan's threat in this regard. By refusing to do so the Government of India has once again favoured its policy of appeasement and surrender towards Pakistan. The party feels that the Kashmir is not the cause but the result, of the India-

Pakistan tension which is inherent, in the very genesis of Pakistan.[45] It thus, appears that the attitude of the Jana Sangh towards Pakistan was in striking contrast to those of the other opposition parties.[46]

Speaking at Ahmedabad, Prof Balraj Madhok said that in the past there was no major war between India and China because of China's adherence to Buddhism which originated in India and the existence of a buffer State of Tibet between the two countries. This geographical distance and cultural proximity were two historical basis of Indo-China friendship in the past.[47] But, with the rise of communism in China and the Chinese occupation of Tibet with Indian acquiescence, the cultural link was broken and the geographical distance eliminated. And now Red China has become India's natural rival as interest of India and China clash in the economic field, in the political field and also in the ideological field.[48] And thus China has become India's enemy and Jana Sangh has no doubt that She (China) is going to remain so for a long time to come.[49] Operating on the traditional principle of diplomacy that enemy of your enemy is your natural friend, India's two enemies—Pakistan and Red China—have become friends and they are going to remain as friends.[50] And therefore, India, according to the Jana Sangh, should adopt a long term strategy to counteract the Sino-Pakistan collusion.

Jana Sangh feels that Communist China poses a threat not only to India and South-East Asia but to Communist countries like Soviet Russia too.[51] Therefore, the party advocates that the cooperation of all countries which subscribe to peace and co-existence should be sought to counteract Red China's expansionist and militaristic policies.[52] For this purpose, the party thinks that the liberation of Tibet, Xinjiang and both Mongolias, the recognition of the Formosa Government and neutralization of South-East Asian countries from the influence of Communist China are necessary.[53] Prof Balraj Madhok said that only an economically and militarily strong India can attract friends in South-East Asia.[54] Jana Sangh also wants to adopt an attitude of impartiality in the Arab-Israel dispute.

About the USA, and USSR, Prof Balraj Madhok said that Jana Sangh would like to remain friendly with both. But, at the same time, Jana Sangh warns that none of them can be our true and eternal friends and we must avoid too much dependence on either of them, because neither of them wants India to become a great power.[55]

Jana Sangh views that "neither our government has been able to curb Pakistan's hostility towards India, nor has it succeeded in making China vacate its aggression from occupied Indian territory. Our policy of international peace not withstanding, no major country supported our just stand on Kashmir."[56] Prof Balraj Madhok would blame India's policy of non-alignment for lack of friends to India. He says, "actually the main objective of the foreign policy is to make friends. But when you say we are non-aligned, that means we arc friendly to none. Then who will be friendly to you? In fact this word non-alignment is the very anti-thesis of foreign relation."[57] Therefore, Atal Bihari Vajpayee, President of the Jana Sangh is of the opinion that India should form an alliance with Japan and Australia to protect the interests of the region but such a link should be with economic cooperation.[58]

Economic Policy

In the economic field, the Jana Sangh stands for what it calls the revival of the spirit of Swadeshi. It says that prosperity is not possible without increased production. But we must also insure equitable distribution so that all people have the urge for and where the fruits of prosperity.[59]

The party realizes that for increased production making the economy dynamic, capital formation is necessary. Capital formation requires savings and enterprise. But the living standard of the common people in India is so low that there is hardly any scope for savings. Therefore, the party gives the call to revive the spirit of 'Swadeshi'[60] or self-help plan to maximize production particularly in agriculture, and employment by the best possible utilization of indigenous equipments and existing opportunities.[61] The Party thinks that this will save us from reckless initiation of the West, from unnecessary and excessive dependence on foreign capital and create in us a tendency for restraint and avoidance of conspicuous consumption. This revival is necessary both for arresting inflation and increasing savings.[62] Therefore, the dominant economic slogan of the Jana Sangh in the mid-term election in Bihar in 1969 was *Har Hath ko Kam, Har Khet ko Pani.*[63] Speaking at Ahmedabad, Prof Balraj Madhok, the then president of the Jana Sangh, said, "so far as economic problem is concerned according to Jana Sangh's view, it is basically problem of two things." It is the problem of unemployment. It is the problem of agriculture. Therefore, his prescription was, increase the employment potential to provide work to all, eliminate uneconomic holdings and provide irrigation facilities.[64] Dr Subramanian Swamy in his *Swadeshi Plan,* presented to the 16th All India session of the Jana Sangh held at Patna on December 28, 29 and 30, 1969, says, our planning of the last 22 years has failed on concepts and policy, our planners have not understood the resource dynamics of the Indian economy. Foreign aid, according to Prof Swamy, has considerably harmed the Indian economy by distorting the investment pattern of the plans.[65] Therefore, he concludes that what we need is a Swadeshi plan which does not rely at all on any foreign aid.[66] Jana Sangh does not deny the utility of foreign aid, but says that as foreign aid can hardly be obtained without strings, and as its flow is basically the function of the foreign policy of the aid giving countries, it would be foolish to our plans dependent on foreign aid.

In economic matters, the Jana Sangh steers a middle course between untrammelled Capitalism and undiluted Statism or Communism and it stands for what it calls a pragmatic approach. It accepts state-ownership of basic industries, but in other spheres it favours increased scope for private enterprise, although under state regulation. The Sangh is against the concentration of economic power through nationalization of all means of production,[67] and it favours special encouragement of small scale units of production. Jana Sangh considers the current controversy about public and private sectors as unreal and harmful to national interest. According to the Party, there is more than enough scope, for both private and public enterprise to work hand in hand for the development of economy. What the country really need (SIC) today is national sector in which private enterprise and resources of the state are coordinated and correlated in the interests of maximum, and more efficient production.[68]

A two-day session of the Bharatiya Pratinidhi Sabha held at Chandigarh in July 1970, presented what the *Organiser*, the non-official Jana Sangh weekly, called the Economic Charter of Jana Sangh.[69] At this session, the party according to the *Organiser*, set before itself the immediate objective to build an egalitarian society where the ratio between what the poor and the rich spend on themselves would be 1 to 20 as against the 1 to 3,250 obtained at present, where 27 crore Indians live on ₹ 20 a day and a minister on ₹ 650 a day.[70] The party stands whole-heartedly to implement Article 39 and 41 of the Indian Constitution which ordain that the State shall, in particular, direct its policy towards securing that the citizens, men and women, equally have the right to adequate means of livelihood and the right to work. The party advocates implementation of land reforms ceiling on agricultural land distribution of waste land among the landless, particularly the Harijans and the tribals, the party guarantees for remunerative price on their major crops. In the urban sector the aim of the party is to reduce concentration of urban property diffuse house ownership, Indianize all industries, nationalize import-export trade with communist countries, proper balance between autonomy and answerability of public undertaking and need based minimum wage. The party has called for an immediate end to foreign aid and advocates doing it themselves. The real cause for the government's tragic failure, said the Bharatiya Pratinidhi Sabha, has been the absence of a realistic approach based upon proper understanding of the peculiar characteristics of our national economy.[71]

In the party's blue print for a peaceful economic revolution in the land there is equal emphasis on production as well as distribution. Its motto is a divine directive from the *Atharva Veda* which ordains, i e with a hundred hands produce with a thousand hands distribute.[72] In this way, Jana Sangh comes very near to Socialism. According to a foreign observer, Although 'Socialism' is not mentioned in connection with economic policy and appears to be regarded as a imported, alien doctrine, the policy set forth (in the Jana Sangh programme) is little different from that practical by the Congress or espoused by the Socialist parties. Economic concerns, however, figures far less in Jana Sangh pronouncements that do social and cultural issues.[73]

At least, it can be safely remarked that the Jana Sangh is not allergic to the humanitarian aims of socialism. This is a party which is fast going through transformation. The change began at the Calicut session of the party and the trend was strengthened at Bombay and then at Patna. The result was that a stage came in 1971 when the Jana Sangh manifesto in effect pledged itself to something indistinguishable from democratic socialism.[74]

According to an Indian observer the emphasis in the Jana Sangh manifesto is clearly on economic issues and on problems of development. It is in these fields that this party has changed its outlook quite radically in the past few years. On the language question also, the Jana Sangh has altered its stand sufficiently to make its position acceptable in the south of Vindhyas.[75] AG Noorani, an eminent Muslim lawyer of Bombay and a well known publicist, in one of his regular series of articles in the *March of the Nation* has remarked, "As is well known Atal Bihari Vajpayee, Jana Sangh president, has been at pains to give a socialist bias to his party."[76] Similarly, the *Free Press Journal* in a special article analysed that it is obvious that the Jana Sangh has sought to give two impression that it has transformed itself into a progressive party wedded to secular democratic socialism and quick all-round economic progress. The same paper further remarked, the economic programme of the Jana Sangh is aimed to portray the secular image of the party, and as the champion of the down trodden masses. In effect, the Jana Sangh pledged itself to democratic socialism and secularism. The economic measures envisaged are ambitious and radical.[77] It is clear that Jana Sangh gives top priority to agriculture because near about 70% people depend upon agriculture. It wants to make small scale and cottage industries, the basis of its programme of industrialization. Jana Sangh is of the opinion that to minimize dependence on foreign aid with regard to foreign aid, the government has mortgaged the future of coming generations of the country. So the foreign aid should be subject to certain conditions. Firstly, the country should be able to nationalize any particular concern after it is paid reasonable compensation by the government. Secondly, the foreigners associated with concerns run or patronized by foreign capital should gain Indians, and thirdly, the period of such participation should be fixed, after finishing such period the industry should be controlled by Indians.

Atal Bihari Vajpayee, speaking in Parliament on the resolution regarding review of the Industrial policy observed that small scale industries should be made the basis of industrialization in our country, and that coordination between the large and small scale industries should be brought about. He said, it is suggested that it is not enough to help small scale industries. The fields of production should be decided upon in such a way that small scale industries may develop in an unhampered manner. To end the competition between the small scale and large scale sectors their spheres of production should be clearly demarcated.[78] Jana Sangh was of the opinion that the government has no price policy. I had failed in establishing prices. So Jana Sangh gave the following suggestions in connection with the rising prices.

1. Threats to nationalize and thus monopolies trade in food grains should stop.
2. One fair price shop for every Gram Sabha unit or per every unit with 1,000 population should be opened.
3. The government should guarantee that families with a monthly income up to ₹ 300, peasants with uneconomic holdings and landless labourers secure a definite and adequate quota from these fair price shops.
4. For government employees and for employees in organized industries instead of increasing DA arrangement should be made to provide them with consumer goods at subsidized rates so as to neutralize the rise in prices.
5. The Zonal scheme should be scrapped forthwith.
6. Sales tax and Octroi duty on food stuffs should be abolished.

7. The government should have forward trading with the farmers.
8. The government should curtail deficit financing.
9. A price stabilization board should be established to regulate the margin of profits.
10. The government should prescribe severe penalties for profit and hoarding.

It is necessary to effect drastic economic in the government's expenditure and to increase the supply of consumer goods.[79]

Jana Sangh advocated following measure for development of small scale industry—

1. Making of machines for cottage and village industries so that their scale of production and income may be increased. Priority in respect of distribution of electric power will be given to these industries.
2. Establishment of industrial schools for training workers in modern technology.
3. Reservation of markets for small scale, cottage and village industries.[80]

In the field of industry, the Jana Sangh stood for the constitution of autonomous corporations to run the different public enterprises. They should be kept free of political interference and control. Jana Sangh wanted to make small and cottage industries the basis of its programme of industrialization.[81]

Bank Nationalization

The Bharatiya Jana Sangh was opposed to Bank nationalization because to it this notion was nothing but a leap in the dark. It is opposed to nationalization of banks on several grounds as fellows—

Firstly, it was not intended to give a new direction to India's economy. It was required to serve only as an ideological cover for factional ambitions.

Secondly, the credit needs of agriculture and small scale sector were not being sufficiently met; there was need for taking steps to give a new direction to the banking industry and ensure a larger flow of capital into these fields.

Thirdly, the progressives are wrong in believing that nationalization is the only alternative to private capitalism. There can be various other alternatives. Cooperativization and municipalization are fairly well known. In case of private factories or industries which are due to be taken over by the government, it is worthwhile to encourage workers within the factory or industry to run their concerns.[82] Therefore, Nationalization was a misnomer to party.

Fourthly, the Jana Sangh rejected both Capitalism as well as Statism. The evils flowing from Private monopoly can be checked through state regulation. But concentration of political as well as economic authority in the hands of the state would result in totalitarianism which is incompatible with democracy.[83]

Fifthly, nationalization is a symbol of bureaucratization. The result of the working of public sector undertaking in India is not happy. The bureaucrats at the helps of public enterprises have neither business acumen nor any appreciable knowledge of industrial psychology.

Jana Sangh favoured to nationalize all foreign banks operating in India and Indianize all foreign-owned consumer goods industries in India.

Jana Sangh was wedded to an ideology of Akhand Bharat. Akhand Bharat was viewed with many ramifications. According to Deendayal Upadhyaya, Akhand Bharat is not only the expression of the geographical unity of the country but also indicates the Bharatiya view of life which manifests unity in diversity. Hence, Akhand Bharat is not some political slogan of ours, accepted because of its popularity under special conditions, but the very basis of our ideology. Many people are doubtful whether Akhand Bharat could ever be achieved. Their doubt is the result of their defeatist mentality. The history of the last half-a-century and the failure of our efforts have so overwhelmed them that they have now lost the heart to rise. In 1947, they saw the failure of their efforts for unity and the success of separation. They lost courage and now wish to make their failure an accepted fact. But this will not be. They cannot go against the genius of the nation. If they do, it will mean suicide. The trials and tribulations of the last six years have this as their reason. The defeat of 1947 was not the defeat of the realization of Bharatiya Unity. It was the defeat of those particular efforts that were made in the name of national unity. We failed not because our goal was wrong but because our means were wrong.[84]

Pakistan naturally occupies a position of vital importance in the ideology of Akhand Bharat. The part maintained that the partition of India was a tragic folly which has served no purpose and had not helped to solve any problem: economic, political and communal. Hence the ultimate ideal of Bharatiya Jana Sangh was Akhand Bharat, that is, the reunion of India and Pakistan. The Bharatiya Jana Sangh did not accept the present division of the subcontinent as permanent. It holds that the very genesis of Pakistan is such that so long as it exists, it will continue to be hostile towards India. As Pakistan cannot be mended it must be ended. Hence, Akhand Bharat is the solution. The Bharatiya Jana Sangh highly criticized the Indus water Treaty. According to the party the treaty was unjust and prejudicial to India's interests. The interests of India, the demands of her security and of her development needs were sacrificed by giving rail links between the two wings. It seems that Government of India is more anxious to supply waters to western Punjab than to Rajasthan and Haryana. The Bharatiya Jana Sangh demanded that any agreement on canal water must provide for immediate diversion of waters of the Indian rivers still being given to Pakistan for use at home. The agreement must not entail any financial responsibility for building canals in Pakistan which are and must remain Pakistan's own responsibility. If India is made responsible at all, a part of its cost must be set off against the debt Pakistan owes to India.[85]

Referring to the talk for a new image for Jana Sangh, Atal Bihari Vajpayee the party president said that in India politics right and left had no meaning. If it had, the Jana Sangh was a middle of the road party. We are committed to social and economic justice and equality. We are committed to the welfare of the people; we are not *status quo* party. He advocates a politics of Indianization, radicalization and modernization for India.[86] Vajpayee said that the Jana Sangh was opposed to socialism to the extent that it was out of date and incomplete. We must fight for getting land for the landless. The Jana Sangh believes in the concept of, "to each according to his need and from each according to his capacity." It is not a Marxist concept but has been the basis of the traditional Indian joint family system.[87]

It can thus be safely remarked that the Sangh is studiously trying to refurbish its image as a progressive democratic party committed to mass welfare and social justice but at the same time insisting on deriving inspiration from all that is great honourable and sublime in Indian culture.

References

1. Bharatiya Jana Sangh, *Principles and Policy: Adopted by the Bharatiya Pratinidhi Sabha* at Vijayawada (Andhra) on January 25 and 26, 1965 (Delhi, Arjun Press), p 3.

2. *Ibid*, pp 1-2.
3. *Ibid*, p 2.
4. *Ibid*, p 3.
5. Jagdish Prasad Mathur, A Historical Glance at Jana Sangh, *The Sunday Searchlight* (Patna) December 28, 1969, p 1.
6. Bharatiya Jana Sangh, *Principles and Policy*, *op cit*, p 6.
7. *Ibid*, p 7.
8. *Ibid*, p 6.
9. See Pandit Deendayal Upadhyaya, *Integral Humanism* (New Delhi, Central Office of the Bharatiya Jana Sangh). Its Principles were accepted by the Gwalior Convention of the Party in 1964.
10. See Bharatiya Jana Sangh: Presidential Address of Atal Bihari Vajpayee at the 16th All India session held at Patna on December 28-30, 1969, pp 10-11
11. *Bharatiya Jana Sangh: A Brief Outline of Policies* (Delhi, Arjun Press).
12. *Principles and Policies*, *op cit*, p 14.
13. *Ibid*.
14. *Ibid*, p 15.
15. *Ibid*, p 16.
16. *Ibid*, p 5.
17. *Ibid*, p 16.
18. *Ibid*, p 17.
19. *Ibid*.
20. Bharatiya Jana Sangh: Presidential Address of Atal Bihari Vajpayee at Patna, December 1969, p 30. *See also* Prof Balraj Madhok, *Indianization: What, How, and Why* (New Delhi, S Chand & Company, June 1970).
21. Vajpayee, *op cit*, p 29. Vajpayee approvingly quoted MRA Baig as follows: "the question, today, before the Muslims is of identity, with whom should they identity themselves their co-religionists or their compatriots? In fact, are they Indian Muslims or Muslim Indians? As they stand at cross roads, between tradition and realism, they face indeed a hard and difficult choice. Tradition points clearly to their

co-religionists. Realism equally indicates that their minds and hearts should be in India rather than in West Asia (*Ibid*, p 32). The only effective remedy for this is to launch a concerned programme of nationalizing the outlook of Indian Muslim said Pandit Premnath Dogra in his presidential address in 1954.

22. Prof Balraj Madhok, *What Bharatiya Jana Sangh Stands For*; speech undertaken by the Ahmedabad Junior Chamber, Ahmedabad, 1966), p 42. The Jana Sangh explains the term Indianization as follows; Indianization by which we mean the subordination of all narrower loyalties like those of religion, caste, region, language or dogma to the overriding loyalty to the nation of all fissiparous elements, especially of those with extra-territorial loyalties or allegiance, over or covert, to the two-nation or multi-nation theory. See AG Noorani, "The Jana Sangh's Indianization", *The Indian Express* (Delhi), May 22 and 30, 1970, p 6.
23. *Principles and Policies*, *op cit*, p 18.
24. *Ibid*, p 24.
25. *Ibid*, p 25.
26. Prof Balraj Madhok, *What Bharatiya Jana Sangh Stands For*, *op cit*, p 17.
27. *Ibid*, p 15.
28. *Ibid*.
29. Prof Balraj Madhok, *What Bharatiya Jana Sangh Stands For*, *op cit*, p 14.
30. *Ibid*.
31. Balraj Madhok, *Selected Speeches in the Lok Sabha* (Delhi, Deepak Prakashan), p 13.
32. Syama Prasad Mukherjee, *Presidential Address at the Founding Convention of the Jana Sangh* held at Delhi on October 21, 1951, *see also* Manifestoes of 1958 and 1962.
33. *Principles and Policy*, *op cit*, p 25.
34. *Ibid*.
35. *Ibid*.
36. *Ibid*. This feeling finds echo in the words of Ramdhari Singh 'Dinkar', a great Hindi poet.
37. Jagadish Prasad Mathur, *op cit*.
38. *Principles and Policy*, *op cit*, pp 25-26.

39. *Ibid*, p 26.
40. Prof Balraj Madhok, *What Jana Sangh Stands For*, *op cit*, p 9.
41. *Ibid*.
42. Prof Balraj Madhok, *Selected Speeches*, *op cit*, p 13.
43. *Principles and Policy*, *op cit*, p 26.
44. Bachhraj Vyas, Presidential Address, 1965.
45. Speaking at a big BJS rally outside the Pakistan High Commission, New Delhi, Prof Madhok said, I am warning the rulers of Pakistan. If they do not cede territory for the resettlement of Hindus thrown out of East Bengal, we shall take it by force, *Organiser*, July 4, 1970, p 3.
46. Resolutions of the Working Committee of the Jana Sangh held at Patna, December 1964.
47. *Ibid*.
48. K Raman Pillai, *India's Foreign Policy* (Meerut, Meenakshi Prakashan, 1969), p 84.
49. Prof Balraj Madhok, *What Bharatiya Jana Sangh Stands For*, *op cit*, p 11
50. *Ibid*.
51. *Ibid*, p 15
52. *Ibid*, p 12
53. *Principles and Policy*, *op cit*, p 26
54. *Ibid*.
55. *Ibid*.
56. *What Bharatiya Jana Sangh Stands For*, *op cit*, p 18.
57. *Ibid*, p 20.
58. *Election Manifesto*, 1962.
59. *What Jana Sangh Stands For*, *op cit*, pp 16-17.
60. See Vajpayee's Press conference at Hong Kong, reported by BK Tiwari, Express News Service, *The Indian Express* (Delhi) July 6, 1970, p 7.
61. *Principles and Policy*, *op cit*, p 27.
62. *Ibid*, p 28.
63. *What Bharatiya Jana Sangh Stands For*, *op cit*, pp 24-33.
64. *Principles and Policy*, *op cit*, p 28.

65. It means; "Work for Every Hand, Water, for Every Field".
66. *What Bharatiya Jana Sangh Stands For*, *op cit*, pp 24-27.
67. Subramanian Swamy, Swadeshi Plan (Central Office, Bharatiya Jana Sangh, New Delhi, 1969), p 24.
68. *Ibid*.
69. *Bharatiya Jana Sangh: A Brief Introduction* (Delhi, Central Office of the Bharatiya Jana Sangh), p 3. See also Important Economic Resolutions, 1952-1957 (Delhi, Central Office of the Bharatiya Jana Sangh). *Manifestoes and Programmes of the Bharatiya Jana Sangh* (Delhi, Central Office of the Bharatiya Jana Sangh, 1956), *Election Manifestoes*, 1957, 1962, and 1967 (Delhi, BJS Office), *Presidential Addresses* (Delhi, BJS Office) etc.
70. *Bharatiya Jana Sangh: A Brief Outline of Politics* (Delhi, Arjun Press), p 5.
71. See the *Organiser* (Delhi), Vol XXIII, No 50, July 25, 1970, p 1.
72. *Ibid*.
73. *Ibid*.
74. *Ibid*.
75. Angela S Burger, *Opposition in a Dominant Party System: A study of the Jana Sangh, The Praja Socialist Party and the Socialist Party in Uttar Pradesh, India* (Bombay, Oxford University Press, by arrangement with the University of California at Berkeley, USA, 1969), p 35.
76. Editorial article entitled "War on Poverty", *The Indian Express* (New Delhi). Vol XXXIV, No 63, January 20, 1971, p 6.
77. *Ibid*.
78. AG Noorani, "Mid-Term Poll and Policy Issues", *March of Nation* (Bombay, edited by Piloo Mody, MP), Vol VIII, No 44, January 9, 1971, p 7.
79. See "Jana Sangh War on Poverty", *The Free Press Journal* (Bombay), 22 January 1971.
80. Lok Sabha Debates (5 August 1960), Cols. 1194 to 1198.
81. Bharatiya Jana Sangh, Resolutions passed by the Bharatiya Pratinidhi Sabha on August 1964, Gwalior (Madhya Pradesh) in BHS Economic Policy Resolutions of Bharatiya Jana Sangh (Bombay: Rajmuntra, 1969), pp 85-87.

82. Bharatiya Jana Sangh, Election Manifesto 1962 (Delhi: Bharatiya Jana Sangh Publication, 1962), p 19.
83. Atal Bihari Vajpayee, speaking in Parliament on the resolution regarding review of the Industrial Policy observed that small-scale industries should be made the basis of industrialization in our country, and that coordination between the large and small scale industries should be brought about. He said, "it is my suggestion that it is not enough to help small scale industries. The fields of production should be decided upon in such a way that small scale industries may develop in an unhampered manner. To end the competition between the small scale and large scale sectors, their spheres of production would be clearly demarcated".

    Lok Sabha Debates (5 August 1960), Cols.
84. Bharatiya Jana Sangh, *Jana Sangh on Bank Nationalization* (Delhi, Navchetan Press), p 14.
85. Bharatiya Jana Sangh, Resolutions passed by the All India Working Committee at Raipur on 1-4 July 1969 and New Delhi on 30-31 August and 1 September 1969 (Delhi: Navchetan Press, 1969), p 6.
86. Deendayal Upadhyaya, *Organiser*, August 24, 1953.
87. Bharatiya Jana Sangh, Resolutions adopted by the Bharatiya Pratinidhi Sabha and the Bharatiya Karya Samiti of Bharatiya Jana Sangh, Poona, 27 June to 8 July 1959 (Delhi: Arjun Press, 1959), p 11.
88. Vajpayee's call "The Indian Export", July 5, 1971, 9.7.
89. *Ibid.*

CHAPTER 4

Kashmir Problem

The Kashmir Problem brought India and Pakistan on the brink of war several times. This occurred in 1947, and more fiercely in 1965. In the 1971 War also, Kashmir inevitably became a scene of armed showdown between India and Pakistan, even though the main battle-field was Bangladesh. Kashmir question generated a state of tension between India and Pakistan, even 25 years after the exit of the British power from this subcontinent. It proved to be the greatest and the gravest single problem between India and Pakistan. Naturally it became the pivot of the relations between the two countries.

Facts about Kashmir

The State of Jammu and Kashmir was founded by Maharaja Gulab Singh in the year 1946.[1] By diplomatic skill and military conquest, Maharaja Gulab Singh consolidated Dogra power over the whole of Kashmir Valley, Gilgit, Baltistan and Ladakh, as well as on Jammu.

The area was inhabited by different communities among whom there was a lack of communication and unity. The mountainous character of the country and the paucity of communications compelled the different communities to continue to live a separate existence.[2]

In size the Jammu and Kashmir is equal to that of Great Britain, covering an area of 86,023 sq. miles. It was the largest of the former princely states of India and according to the 1941 census, it had a population of about 40 lakhs, 77% of them being Muslims, 20% Hindus and 3% Sikhs, Buddhist and other minorities. It occupies a highly strategic position. It is bounded in the north by Afghanistan, Russia and China and in the west and south by Pakistan and in the south and south east by India in the east by Tibet.

The Kashmir Valley has predominantly Muslim population while Jammu region has a predominantly Hindu population. The State of Jammu and Kashmir prior to 1947 was governed by the doctrine of Paramount, under which British Sovereignty rule supreme particularly in matters of external affairs, defence and communications. Paramount symbolized the supremacy of British power over all princely states in India and allegiance of the Princely rulers to the British crown.

Butler Committee did no define paramount, it was living, growing relationship shaped by constantly changing circumstances and policy, deriving its strength from mixture of history, theory and modern facts. In the world of the Butler Committee, paramount had to adopt itself

> "according to the shifting necessities of the time and the progressive development of the State."[3]

The Cabinet Missions memorandum of 12 May 1946 said that on transfer of power

> "His Majesty's Government will cease to exercise powers of paramount. This means that the rights of the states which flow from their relationship with the Crown will no longer exist and that all the rights surrendered by the states to the paramount power will return to the States."[4]

MA Jinnah the Governor-General designate of the dominion of Pakistan, interpreted this as regaining sovereign status by the princely states. In a statement of 30 July 1947 he said that,

> "the Legal position is that with the lapse of paramount on the transfer of power by the British, all Indian states would automatically regain the fully sovereign and independent status."[5]

Lord Mountbatten, the British Viceroy, had told the princely rulers on 25 July 1947 that

> "The Indian Independence Act releases the States from all their obligations to the Crown. The States have complete freedom technically. Legally they are independent."

However, he added in the same breath,

> "you cannot run away from the dominion government which is your neighbour any more then you can run away from the subject for whose welfare you are responsible."[6]

The All India Congress Committee in a resolution on 15 June 1957 had held that "the lapse (of paramount) does not lead to the independence of the states" and said "it is clear that the people of the States must have dominating voice in any decision regarding them.[7]

The Kashmir Government under Maharaja Hari Singh had concluded a Standstill Agreement with the Government of Pakistan in regard to the maintenance of the existing arrangement in respect of post and telegraph, etc.

He took time to decide on joining either India or Pakistan. As the Maharaja said in the letter to Lord Mountbatten on 26 October 1947,

> "Geographically my state is contiguous to both the Dominions. It has vital economic and cultural link with both of them. I wanted to take time to decide to which Dominion I should accede, whether it is not in the best interest of both the dominions and my state to stand independent, of course, with friendly and cordial relations with both."[8]

In violation of the Standstill Agreement, Pakistan Government stopped supply of food and other essential goods and sent soldiers in plain clothes with Afridies and Desperados with modern weapons and they unleashed a reign to loot, and destruction of life and property and kidnapping and dishonouring of women.

In those circumstances, Maharaja Hari Singh had "no option but to ask for help to Indian Dominion."

As India could not send the help asked for without the state acceding to the Dominion of India, therefore, the Maharaja decided to accede his state to the Indian Union and signed the Instrument of Accession. The other alternative before him was to leave his state to the looters.

India accepted the Instrument of Accession and Jammu and Kashmir became a part of India.

India air-lifted troops to Srinagar, and thus, it became a confrontation between India and Pakistan. At the same time, India referred Kashmir question to the United Nations Security Council under Article 35 of the United Nations Charter and accused Pakistan of adding and abetting the invaders against Kashmir and requested the Security Council to call upon Pakistan to refrain from such actions.[9]

In a lengthy reply, Pakistan said that Kashmir Accession to India was achieved by fraud and violence and that India was persistently attempting to undo the partition scheme and destroy the state of Pakistan.[10]

India's Stake, Pakistan's Stake

Both India and Pakistan have claimed that Kashmir is necessary for the survival of each country. India says that voluntarily accession of Jammu and Kashmir, with its preponderant Muslim majority would vindicate and strengthen the secular nationalism of India. India says that the partition of the country in 1947 was based on the principle of political expediency and not on the acceptance of the 'pernicious' two-nation theory of the late MA Jinnah. The logical consequence of acceptance of the two-nation theory would be to render the sizeable Muslim population in India to the status of non-nationals. This cannot be accepted because it will not only inflict inhuman injustice on the Muslims but would also lead to the inevitable fragmentation of India on grounds of religious minorities.

India is a country with many religions, culture and languages. To consider Muslims as a separate nation on the basis of their separate religion would also entitle the followers of other religions for similar demands.

On the other hand, Kashmir, remaining with India would mean a victory of India's secularism and territorial nationalism. It would have progressive and modernizing effect. This is in consonance with the world wide trend of thinking and development.

India says that it accepted Pakistan as separate state and wished it all progress, but it cannot accept the retrogressive theory of religious nationalism.

Apart from the ideological argument, India also advances to cleanse legal argument. It says that under the Indian Independence Act, 1947, it was the ruler of a princely state who was given power to decide the future of his state. The Maharaja of Jammu and Kashmir Sir Hari Singh voluntarily signed the Instrument of Accession merging his state with the Indian Union.

Although his action was forced by the pressure of Pakistani attack on his state, Pakistan had attacked to force the merger of Jammu and Kashmir with the Pakistani Union. But it had the opposite effect. For this only Pakistan is to be blamed. Thus India has a great stake in Jammu and Kashmir.

Further, the Maharaja's action was supported by the National Conference, the biggest representative political party of the State, and has been confirmed by the people in several general elections and has been certified by the Constituent Assembly of the State.

On the other hand Pakistan also advances similar arguments to strengthen its claim over Jammu and Kashmir, It says that Pakistan was founded on the principle that Muslim majority areas of British India should be gripped together to form Pakistan, because they are a separate nation. This principle was implemented not only in western provinces of British India but has also in the distantly situated East Bengal and Silhat. Its implementation has been held up in Jammu and Kashmir by India. The merger of Jammu and Kashmir with Pakistan would be the victory of Muslim nationalism. On the other hand, denial of Pakistani sovereignty over Jammu and Kashmir will strengthen other provinces of Pakistan in their demand for their independent existence outside Pakistan. This would lead to the destruction of Pakistan.

Pakistan says that India is following double standard. In case of Junagarh, whose Nawab declared the accession of his state to Pakistan, India insisted on ascertaining the will of the people, because of majority of Junagarh is formed by the Hindus, whereas in case of Jammu and Kashmir, India is insisting on the formal power of the ruler to decide the future of his state. Pakistan demands free and fair plebiscite under an impartial international supervision.

Thus Pakistan claims that it has vital stake in Jammu and Kashmir and that it remains incomplete till Jammu and Kashmir is allowed to join Pakistan.

India and Pakistan have fought three major wars on the soil of Jammu and Kashmir and several legal battles at the United Nations. In fact, the relationship between India and Pakistan has been conditioned by their conflict over the question of Jammu and Kashmir. There was a protected armed show down between the two countries in 1947-48 till a cease-fire was affected under the United Nations' supervision. Having failed to grab Kashmir by force, Pakistan joined American military alliance. It got huge quantity of American arms and stated preparing for an occasion to occupy Kashmir by force.

Pandit Jawaharlal Nehru died on 27 May 1964 and India was deprived of the benefits of his towering leadership. India was also militarily unprepared. It was licking the wounds inflicted by defeat and humiliation at the hands of China in 1962 boarder conflict. It was at this time that Pakistan attacked India but even in this war Pakistan failed to achieve its objective and under the 'Tashkent Declaration' of 1966 it had to promise the adjure violence to settle any dispute with India. In affect it meant forgetting Kashmir.

Their third war fought in 1971, although the immediate provocation was provided by Pakistani atrocities in what is today Bangladesh. This resulted in humiliating defeat of Pakistan and separation of East Pakistan and Its emergence into an independent Bangladesh.

After 1971, ZA Bhutto became Prime Minister of remaining part of Pakistan.

He signed an agreement with India, known as the Simla Pact, on 2 July 1972 under which both India and Pakistan "resolved to settle their differences by peaceful means." He also committed his country to the position

> "that pending the final settlement of any of the problems between the two countries, neither side shall unilaterally alter the situation and both shall prevent the organization,

> assistance or encouragement of any act detrimental to the maintenance of peaceful and harmonious relations."

Further, the Simla Pact provided both India and Pakistan

> "shall always respect each other's national unity, territorial integrity, political independence and sovereign equality ... they will refrain from the threat or use of force against the territorial integrity or political independence of each other, both governments will take all steps within their 'power to prevent hostile propaganda' directed against each other."[11]

This pact was welcomed in India because it symbolized Pakistan's implicit agreement to the maintenance of the *status quo* in Kashmir and respect for the continued Indian sovereignty over major part of Jammu and Kashmir.

In spite of this agreement it cannot be said that Pakistan is fully reconciled to the present position in Kashmir. For example in October 1976 the Pakistan delegate in the UN Social and Humanitarian Committee tried to harp on the old UN resolution calling for a plebiscite in Kashmir to decide its future status. A few days ago the leader of the Pakistan delegation, Aziz Ahmad had made a similar attempt in the UN General Assembly. The Indian delegate, Margaret Alva drew the Pakistan delegate's attention to the need for adhering to the frame work and spirit of the Simla Pact and avoiding polemics. She declared

> "there would be no question of the Jammu and Kashmir people exercising the right of self-determination in a manner separate from the destiny of India that would be violation of the sovereignty and territorial integrity of India and an unwarranted interference in the internal affairs of India, thereby constituting violation of UN Charter."

She further pointed out that the problem that still remained was the continued and illegal occupation by Pakistan of two-fifths of the Indian territory of Jammu and Kashmir. This question of Pakistan's aggression, Alva said,

> "has to be resolved through bilateral talks within the framework and in the spirit of the Simla Agreement."

She said that the old UN resolutions on Jammu and Kashmir had become obsolete following Pakistan's failure to fulfil the essential preconditions laid down in them. This was specifically pointed out by the late Pandit Nehru on 5 June 1949 that Pakistan's failure to implement the resolution of 1948,

> "would render India free of any obligation which it might have voluntarily accepted."[12]

This was a Pakistani attempt to hammer the controversy on Jammu and Kashmir. In April 1978 Agha Shahi, Foreign Affairs Adviser to the President of Pakistan, again tried to take up the Kashmir issue which was replied by Atal Bihari Vajpayee, India's Minister for External Affairs, on the lines adopted by Alva in 1976.

Attitude of Jana Sangh Towards Kashmir Question

The main issue of the Jana Sangh since its birth has been Pakistan and the invasion on Kashmir and continued Pakistani occupation over a part of the state. Jana Sangh believed in Akhand Bharat (Undivided India) and accused the Congress government of following a policy of appeasement towards Pakistan. However, so long as Pakistan existed, Jana Sangh advocated a policy of reciprocity towards it.

As its manifesto declared,

> "so long as Pakistan continues to be a separate entity, Jana Sangh will adopt a policy of reciprocity in dealing with that state."[13]

The manifesto further said

> "the policy of appeasement that has so long been followed has not changed the mentality of the leaders of Pakistan; on the contrary it has strengthened it, the Jana Sangh is against giving any concession to Pakistan on the question of evacuating property, recovery of India's loans and canal water dues."[14]

Jana Sangh felt that the partition of the country in 1947 was affected on an unnatural basis. Therefore, it has not solved any problem. Rather it has tended to aggravate the existing problems and has created tension in the Indian subcontinent.

> "Our approach to these problems is not communal. They are mainly political and economic and they have to be settled between the two countries in straight forward manner."[15]

Jana Sangh was very critical of the policy pursued by Pandit Nehru towards Pakistan, because in its view, Nehru's policy suffered from "a lack of national approach,"[16] and was based on a blind policy of appeasement.

In its view Pakistan was following a devilish policy of oppression of Hindu minorities in Pakistan and was best on squeezing them out automatically ever since this Islamic state came in to being. India under Pandit Nehru did nothing affective. On the other hand, it blamed, Pandit Nehru for his 'appeasement and hush-hush operation' of unwelcome facts. Therefore, Jana Sangh advocated a policy of reciprocity and strength towards Pakistan and to give up the policy of what it called 'surrender and appeasement'.

According to it all agreements and settlements between India and Pakistan under Pandit Nehru, India has been looser and Pakistan has been the gainer. As in a resolution the Jana Sangh said,

> "In the most of these settlements, it has been not a case of give and take, it has rather been a case of India giving

> in and Pakistan taking territory or concessions all along. Such settlements are against national interests; and the Bharatiya Jana Sangh accordingly condemned such settlements."[17]

The resolution passed by the Jana Sangh at its Ahmedabad session in 1963 gives a more complete view of the attitude of Jana Sangh towards Pakistan. As Resolution No 3 passed on that occasion said

> "it has been the considered view of Bharatiya Jana Sangh that Pakistan by its very genesis and nature is destined to take India as its enemy number one. So long as it exists, hostility to India and Hindus is the only prop which keeps this artificial state, divided by thousand miles of Indian territory, going. Its continual adventure against India, the continuous anti-India and anti-Hindu outbursts of its rulers and press and constant harassment of its Hindu population, which has been deprived of even its basic human rights and which is being steadily decimated through physical extermination, conversion and forcible expulsion from Pakistan and encouragement of Naga hostiles are manifestations of its policy of keeping the anti-India and Anti-Hindu frenzy at the highest pitch in Pakistan at all times."[18]

The Jana Sangh is convinced that because Pakistan was formed out of hostility towards the Hindus and India, the basis of its continued existence is the pursuit of that policy; Pakistan cannot get rid of its hostility towards India.

If India makes one concession to Pakistan, Pakistan will come forward with another demand. Jana Sangh thinks that the Kashmir problem is not the cause of Pakistan's hostility towards India rather it is the result of Pakistan's hostility as the Jana Sangh resolution said

> "it would be wrong to hope that Pakistan would change its attitude if Kashmir question was solved, as the so called Kashmir problem is just a fact of Pakistani policy, Pakistan will always whip up some problem or the other, even if the existing Kashmir problem is solved."[19]

The same attitude was expressed by Balraj Madhok in the Lok Sabha on November 1961. He said that

> "Pakistan was born out of hostility towards India and it lives on hostility to India. It knows that the moment that hostility ceases, the moment the country became friendly, there can be no Pakistan as separate State."

According to him,

> "Pakistan is an absurdity which cannot exist. It can only exist if it can continue to be enemy of India."[20]

The *Organiser* echoed the same sentiment in its editorial and it said that Pakistan's hostility to India is incurable. Any concessions to that country from India will only be its appetite.[21]

Such is the clear attitude of Jana Sangh towards Pakistan on other matters of detail of its attitude towards that country follow logically. Jana Sangh advocates no concessions to Pakistan and curbing its capacity to mischief so long as that country exists.

As *Organiser* editorial said,

> "The best way to cure them (Pakistan) of this malady is to purge them of all capacity for mischief. From now on, let India act, and leave Pakistan to react. Let us have the initiative natural to our size and resources."[22]

The attitude of the Jana Sangh towards the Kashmir Question is only a reflection of the more fundamental attitude of the

Party towards Pakistan. The Party thinks that Pakistan has started the dispute over Jammu and Kashmir because it is the very nature of Pakistan to be inimical towards India and that even if the Kashmir question is settled to satisfaction of Pakistan, the latter will pick up some other apple of discord.

Therefore, Jana Sangh's position on the Kashmir question has been somewhat rigid. That is, Kashmir belongs to India by virtue of the Instrument of Accession signed by the then Maharaja of Jammu and Kashmir. Once Kashmir has become part and parcel of India, there can be no question of a plebiscite to determine its future status.

Jana Sangh wants complete integration of Jammu and Kashmir State within the Indian Union and, therefore, it wants to scrap Article 370 of the Indian Constitution, which grants special status to Jammu and Kashmir within the India Union. Jana Sangh thinks that the only problem about Kashmir is the problem of continued Pakistani occupation in an illegal manner of about one-third of the state masquerading as the Azad Kashmir. After 1962 Jana Sangh has also been demanding for the evacuation of the Chinese from the North-Eastern strip of Ladakh which is illegally occupied by China.

Jana Sangh viewed Article 378 of the Indian Constitution as simply an anachronism. It should be abrogated. Its repeal would serve a valuable Psychological purpose. All speculations about Kashmir would automatically stop. The Continuation of a separate constitution, separate flag and separate law of citizenship for Jammu and Kashmir State looked and presented a very dangerous example. It gave inspirations to separatist forces in other parts of the country. It made a mockery of repeated declarations made by India in the United Nations Organization about Jammu and Kashmir State being an integral part of India. Scrapping of the separate constitution of Jammu and Kashmir state and deletion of Article 370 of the Indian constitution would be a more eloquent testimony to Kashmir being an integral part of India than all the resolutions and declarations of the government and its spokesmen to that effect. It was this discriminatory status of the Jammu and Kashmir State which had made many patriotic people of that State feel that they were treated as second class citizens within their own country.[23] From its very inception the Jana Sangh has made the Kashmir problem a very live issue. Its endeavours to channelize events in the right direction have cost it an immeasurable loss—the martyrdom of its founder leader Dr Syama Prasad Mukherjee. But it is owing to this sacrifice that Kashmir has been retained as a part and parcel of India.[24]

The Jana Sangh was of the opinion that the popular discontent had arisen out of regional imbalances in Jammu and Ladakh. There were people who accused the people of these regions as being prompted by communal considerations. The fact was that it was the discrimination against these regions which was grounded on a communal basis. The Kashmir State Government should accept and implement the recommendations of the Gajendragadkar Commission.[25]

The Party considers Pakistan as an implacable enemy of India which can thrive only on the basis of its continued hostility. As in the Lok Sabha Prof Balraj Madhok, once the Party's theoretician said

> "Pakistan was born out of hostility towards India and it lives on hostility for India. It (Pakistan) is an absurdity which cannot exist. Let us realize that so long as Pakistan exists, it will remain an enemy of India, whatever we may do to appease it and to be friends with it. Only a policy of reciprocity can solve the problems. We must have tooth for tooth and eye for eye. That may be a barbaric principle but that is the only language that Pakistan understands."[26]

In April 1958 at the 6th Annual Session of Jana Sangh, Prof DP Ghose said:

> "All these problems of Kashmir and Pakistan and refugees boil down to one thing ... they all traceable to one original sin, the sin of partition of our motherland, the matricide perpetrated ten years ago... until that sinful chapter is closed and the two portions of India are reunited this suffering will continue we shall rest not, nor shall we be weary, in the pursuit of our efforts for the integration of India and the establishment of 'Akhand Bharat'."[27]

According to Jana Sangh, Kashmir is an integral part of India and its accession to India is permanent and irrevocable. Therefore, any talk of plebiscite in Kashmir is useless, illogical and unnecessary. It has suggested that the UNO should be moved to declare Pakistan as an aggressor and all possible steps should be taken for liberation of Azad Kashmir, which was illegally occupied by the Government of Pakistan. Jana Sangh was not in favour of a separate constitution for Jammu and Kashmir. It was totally opposed to Article 370 of the Indian Constitution. The Party demanded that Article 370 of the Constitution of India which was intended to be of a temporary nature, would be immediately abrogated and Jammu and Kashmir State brought as per with the other states of the country.[28]

It wanted full integration of the State within the Union of India and end of its special status as envisaged by Article 370 of the Indian constitution. It also wanted to abrogate the separate constitution of the state. It had launched a civil disobedience struggle in 1953 whose slogan was *"Ek Desh me Vidhan, Ek Pradhan Aur Ek Nishan"* (in one country, there should be only one constitution, one Head of the State and one flag).

The State Government had introduced permit system to regulate and restrict the entry into the State. Dr Syama Prasad Mukherjee, the founder President of the Bharatiya Jana Sangh, led a batch of Satyagrahi into Jammu. He was arrested and was imprisoned at Srinagar, where he died in circumstances which appeared mysterious. The party has projected this event as martyrdom of Dr Syama Prasad Mukherjee for the cause of full integration of Jammu and Kashmir with India.

In fact, the biggest single argument in favour of abrogation of Article 370 at the earliest is the imperative need to eliminate the advantage whose continuance confers upon the pro-Pak and secessionist elements by allowing them to keep alive in a section of the people the feeling that the final word for Kashmir's future still remained to be said. The pro-Pakistani elements would find themselves out of business the day this Article is scrapped and the present state of political indecisiveness, however illusory would come to an end.[29]

The central working committee of BJS has noted with satisfaction that the people of India irrespective of their party affiliations have realised the dangerous implication of continuation of the temporary Article 370 of the Indian Constitution.[30] The unstinted support by all groups and parties in Parliament given to the private bill to abrogate this Article was welcome indication of the nation's mind in this respect. It is clear vindication of the stand the Jana Sangh has taken in this regard from its very inception.

According to Bakshi Ghulam Mohammad, the main cause of retaining Article 370 was that Kashmir was running through peculiar circumstances, no other states of India faced cease-fire line on its soil. It created its own special problems which no other state had. It is to provide special safeguards that Article 370 has been inserted and retained.

Jana Sangh demanded that even after the abrogation of Article 370, the Indian Constitution could very well provide suitable safeguards for the interests and welfare of the people of the Jammu and Kashmir.

It is, however, a matter of deep regret that the Government of India has once again faltered in the matter. It has betrayed its communal and unrealistic approach to these vital issues by insisting on retaining Article 370, which has become the symbol of separatism for the separatist and communal elements in Kashmir, as such. The application of some more Article of the Indian Constitution to that state is good so far as it goes but it loses sight of the basic fact that it will not in any way help in countering the psychological impact of this Article which is the basic hurdle in the way of emotional oneness of Kashmir with the rest of India.

On the other hand, the special status of the state created an anomalous situation and caused havoc with the concept of India unity. An Indian citizen could not enter Kashmir territory without permit and could not purchase land there nor could be a voter. Even Pandit Jawaharlal Nehru, with all his love for Kashmir and his ancestral link with it, was ineligible to be a voter there. The Jana Sangh pointed out that the fact that the rulers of Pakistan feel so much concerned about any move to abrogate this Article is a clear proof of its dangerous import for India. Abrogation of this Article at one stroke could be the only patriotic and practical reply to Pakistan's threats towards India.

But this is not going to satisfy Pakistan, which objects to the very presence of India in Kashmir.[31]

The Party said that it would be more realistic and conducive to ultimate good of all concerned if we let Pakistan howl all at once by abrogating this Article at one stroke rather than keep her howling all the time. This pandering to Pakistan's intransigence blows from the basically wrong presumption that Kashmir is the cause of Indo-Pakistan tension. Kashmir in fact is not the cause but, the result of the tension which is inherent in the very genesis of Pakistan. Therefore, any appeasement of, or compromise with Pakistan at the cost of Kashmir in the ultimate analysis increases rather than lessens the Indo-Pak tension by further whetting the aggressive appetite of Pakistan.

Jana Sangh, therefore, urges upon the Government of India to give up its policy of vacillation about Kashmir of which its present attitude towards the issue of abrogation of Article 370 is the direct result. This Article even it if become an empty shell will continue to be the source of inspiration for the separatist and communal, elements in Kashmir. Therefore, realism and national interests as also expediency demand that this Article must be removed from the Constitution of India; locked, stocked and barrelled; so that the Constitution as a whole may become the Constitution of Jammu and Kashmir State as well. This one step will have more settling effect on the minds of the people of that state than anything else done so far to that end.[32]

Jana Sangh criticized Pandit Nehru's statement made in New York in 1960 on Kashmir in which he had stated that the *status quo* in Kashmir should be maintained. Pandit Nehru's statement, it was pointed out,

> "amounted the India's reconciliations to Pakistani occupation of one-third of Kashmir and an abandonment of our rightful claims over that area."[33]

Pitambar Das said that "even the over-generous gift of canal waters has failed to quench the thirst of Pakistani aggression."[34] It is a fact that in all the treaties and agreements between India and Pakistan, up to date, India had invariably been a loser. It shows that the country's interests will always remain insecure so long as the present government will continue to rule the country.

The party strongly criticized the canal water treaty. Before the Prime Minister left for Pakistan to sign the treaty in

September 1969, it demanded a categorical assurance from him that he would not in any way agree to any infringement of the sovereign right of India in Kashmir. It had demanded the government not to sign the canal water treaty, unless the clause with regard to Mangla Dam in Pakistan-occupied Kashmir, was deleted. Pandit Deendayal Upadhyaya said,

> "Pakistan got all that it wanted and we lost all that was justifiably ours. The surrender of India's territorial and sovereign right is a betrayal which can hardly be tolerated."[35]

Jana Sangh observes that Pandit Nehru, who had been handling Kashmir on behalf of Government of India and treating it almost as a personal affair, began his bungling from that very beginning. The unilateral and illegal offer of plebiscite and its continuous repetition, appeal to the UNO, failure to explicitly name Pakistan an aggressor in the original complaint to UNO, failure to sent right men to plead India's case there, ordering of ceasefire when the Indian troops were advancing on all fronts, failure to settle Hindu refugees uprooted by Pakistani invaders in Kashmir in spite of their repeated requests, failure to exercise affective check on Kashmir administration and incorporation of temporary article 370 in the Indian Constitution to appease Sheikh Abdullah's ambitions were series of the early blunders committed by the Nehru government in regard to Kashmir.[36]

Their natural result was to swell the head of Sheikh Abdullah who began to dream of making Jammu and Kashmir virtually an independent Sheikhdom with a separate constitution, separate flag and separate Head of the State. He might have succeeded in his nefarious desires, but for the opposition of the nationalist and patriotic forces within the State led by Pandit Prem Nath Dogra and the country-wide campaign launched in support of Kashmiri people's just made patriotic demands by the Jana Sangh. The great martyrdom of

Dr Syama Prasad Mukherjee ultimately clinched the issue. The country was awakened and the hands of Pandit Nehru were forced. Sheikh Abdullah was arrested and put in jail and new government was installed in the State. As a result of process of integration of the State with rest of India was set in motion.[37]

The Jana Sangh observe that immediate steps be taken to bring Jammu and Kashmir State completely in line with the rest of India by deleting Article 370 of the Indian Constitution and applying the Constitution to Kashmir also in full. This, the working committee feels, is essential to give an air of reality to the declarations and professions about Kashmir being an integral part of India.[38]

Jana Sangh observes that no useful purpose can be served by keeping the question open for discussion at the UNO. It requests upon the Government to withdraw the Kashmir issue there and desist from wasting any more money, time, and energy in trying to convince those who are determined not to be convinced. It further urges upon the government to take all immediate effective steps to recover possession of the Kashmir territory now aggressively occupied by Pakistan.[39]

After 1965, when Pakistan was humiliated in a war of its own bidding by India, then Bharatiya Jana Sangh demanded not only the liberation of Kashmir and the integration of the entire State of Jammu and Kashmir with India but also gave slogan of liberation of Azad Kashmir.

Jana Sangh feels that India's handling of the Kashmir question involved a series of blunders. According to it, the first blunder in India's handling of the Kashmir Problem was committed just on the day when the historic decision to accept the State's accession and defend her against Pakistani hordes was taken. Pandit Nehru announced without consulting even his cabinet that the question of accession of the State would be finally decided by the people of the State through a plebiscite to be held after Pakistani invaders were pushed out of the State and normal conditions restored.

It is obvious that the offer of plebiscite was totally wrong both from constitutional as well as political point of view. From the constitutional point of view, the decision of the ruler of Kashmir was a final decision. But it was also supported by the major political organizations of his state. Therefore, the question of plebiscite did not arise. Pakistan's policy was based on the path of war so she could not claim plebiscite which is essentially a path of peace. Politically, the step was even wrong because the people of the state did not demand it as a condition precedent to accession.

According to Jana Sangh, the second blunder committed by the Government of India was that the Kashmir Question was referred to the UNO. The records of the UNO have proved that this is a body of power politics and was incapable of doing justice in the case. The reference to the UNO has only resulted in aggravating the problem rather than solving it. The UN Security Council has proved it to be the 'Insecurity Council'.

Jana Sangh was also sore on internal administration of the State, and particularly, the treatment meted out to the Hindu and other minorities there at the hands of the State Government. The Jana Sangh described that the key posts in the State of Jammu and Kashmir are manned by the Muslims. Open competition system for recruiting officers has been denied. Advertisements are bound to say that 'Only Muslims need apply'.

According to our Constitution, Fundamental Rights have been safeguarded by the Supreme Court of India. But in the State of Jammu and Kashmir a large number of political opponents are detained without trial.

The Nehru-Abdullah Agreement of July 1952, provided for a separate constitution, a separate flag, and a Sadar-i-Riyasat.

This virtually made Kashmir, a different State, was a dangerous concession to Sheikh Abdullah. As Madhok told that their persistence in their present policy towards Sheikh Abdullah would surely turn Kashmir into another Pakistan. Let them not create a third nation out of the Indian Nation while fretting and foaming against the two-nation theory.[40]

It was the opinion of Bharatiya Jana Sangh that elimination of Hindu, suppression of civil rights, communalism in services, discrimination against Jammu, vivisection of Jammu on communal lines and double game of Sheikh Abdullah has further aggravated the Kashmir problem.

According to Jana Sangh, the State Government is guilty of gross neglects towards the people of Jammu and Ladakh. Article 335 of the Constitution of India be made applicable to the Jammu-Kashmir State and reservation for the Scheduled Castes made in the service in proportion to their population, other posts should be filled upon the basis of merits.

The agitations for restoring regional balance in favour of Jammu and Ladakh and ensuring justice to them in matters of employment development activities and cultural and educational spheres led to the demand for reorganization of the state and merging of Ladakh with Himachal Pradesh and Jammu with Punjab or Haryana. This led to the appointment of the Gajendragadkar Commission. The Commission recommended some economic and educational safeguards for the people of Jammu and Ladakh and establishment of a separate University at Jammu.

Pandit Jawaharlal Nehru died on 27 May 1964, and Lal Bahadur Shastri succeeded him as India's second Prime Minister. Pakistan was flexing its muscle to settle its old score with India in Kashmir. Pakistan armed to the teeth with latest American weapons. Pakistan launched on the way of military confrontation with India. It first set out to probing India military preparation by occupying a portion of Kutch and laying claim over its major part.[41] The Kutch dispute was pacified by the mediatory role of the British Prime Minister whose suggestion for adjudication of the problem was accepted by both India and Pakistan. In the meanwhile Pakistan sent its armed infiltrators into Jammu-Kashmir and later on sent its army. India declared that any invasion of the line of control of Jammu-Kashmir will be regarded as an invasion on India. As a diversionary tactics, India sent its forces towards Lahore and Sialkot to relieve the pressure of Pakistani attack on Jammu.

The armed showdown resulted in a stalemate, although India succeeded in capturing the Haji Pir pass and several important Pakistani military posts. The Indian Army reached on the outskirts of Lahore and Sialkot. At the mediation of Russian Prime Minister, the Tashkent Pact was signed between India and Pakistan. This pact provided for restoration of antebellum in return of Pakistani promise of renunciation of force to settle Kashmir problems in future. But the conclusion the Tashkent pact also witnessed the sad and premature death of the Indian Prime Minister Lal Bahadur Shastri.

The Tashkent declaration was criticized by the Jana Sangh. The Party observed that the declaration is no assurance of stable, of real peace between India and Pakistan. Pakistan has refused to agree to any categoric no-war pact and has just reaffirmed faith in the provisions of the UN Charter rewriting that force be adjusted in the settlement disputes. The membership of the UNO and the obligations imposed by its Charter on Pakistan have not prevented in from mounting an aggression on Indian thrice in eighteen years in a bid to have things settled by force. Pakistan's argument for the rejection of the no-war proposal clearly shows that it is in no way prepared to renounce use of force until the Kashmir problem is settled in its favour. It would, therefore, be indulging in self-delusion to think that the Tashkent declaration means the end of Pakistan's aggressive intentions.[42]

Jana Sangh had expected that at the Tashkent parlays, India would seek to secure the complete vacation of Pakistan's aggression in Kashmir. But for doing this, India agreed to withdraw to the '5th August line'. Thus, India would be quitting an area which is legally and constitutionally an integral part of Indian territory, and which have been liberated from Pakistan's clutches by our brave jawans at a heavy price. This decision also goes counter to the solemn assurances given to the people. The occupation of these areas had become imperative for two-fold strategic reasons as well.[43]

The entry of infiltrators into Jammu-Kashmir State had to be plugged and China's threat in Ladakh had to be effectively checkmated. Pakistan has not accepted any responsibility for the infiltrators in the State nor given any assurance that it would resume infiltration and sabotage activities again.

There is no evidence either that the Sino-Pak collaboration against India is going to end. Even while the Tashkent talks were in progress, China sent its troops into the demilitarised zone and in a note reiterated its preposterous agreeing to withdraw to the 5th August line was not only wrong in principle but was fought with grave danger for national security.[44]

The interpretation being put on the Tashkent declaration by Pakistani spokesman clearly reveals their intentions. President Ayub's statement showed that he regarded the agreement only as a stepping stone for the fulfilment of Pakistan's ambitions on Kashmir like the several other Indo-Pak pacts agreed to earlier, this also would only serve to what Pakistan's aggressive appetite, the party held.

This central working committee of BJS regretted that to sell this by agreement to the people, attempts were made to exploit the tragedy of Shastriji's sad and sudden death. It was necessary that the declaration be objectively analysed and its far-reaching implications understood.[45]

During 1965 war, the Jana Sangh members helped Indian government by taking up several civilian assignments like regulating traffic, providing transport, medical assistance, clothes etc, for the jawans. The Jana Sangh had opposed the Kutch Agreement as well as the Tashkent Pact, and turned them as capitulation of the Indian government before the Pakistani intransigence.

Jana Sangh was very much against returning the Pakistani military posts captured by India during the war, and it wanted that Government of India should cease upon that opportunity to fully integrate Kashmir with the rest of India. This would have settled the Kashmir problem for ever. As Prof Balraj Madhok observed,

> "had the Government of India taken advantage of this situation to fully integrate Kashmir with the rest of India and had it extended Indian Constitution to enable the people from other parts of the country to settle there, the danger of Pakistan designs on Kashmir would have been effective by scotched forever."[46]

In 1971 the relations between East Pakistan and West Pakistan deteriorated to the flesh point. The Awami League under the leadership of Sheikh Muzibur Rahman had registered a sweeping victory in East Pakistan and had got a majority in the Pakistan National Assembly in the first-ever General Election held in Pakistan. The triumph of Sheikh Muzibur Rahman was not acceptable to political and military leaders, who counted in West Pakistan. Pakistan resorted to an armed crack down in East Pakistan and millions of refugees were driven to India.

Finally Pakistan declared a war on India. The war resulted in dismemberment of East Pakistani troops surrendered at the hand of India in Dacca and a few square miles of Pakistani territory in Pakistan was captured by India.

Also India succeeded in straightening the line of control of Jammu-Kashmir by capturing several Pakistani posts while Pakistan succeeded in occupying sixty square miles of Chamb area in Jammu, part of India. India thus achieved a convincing victory.

However, India signed a Simla Pact with Pakistan, Article 4 of the Agreement provided

> "in Jammu-Kashmir the line of control resulting from the case file of 17 December 1971 shall be respected by both sides without prejudice to the recognise position of the either side. Neither side shall seek to alter it unilaterally irrespective of mutual differences and legal interpretations. Both sides further undertake to refrain from the threat or use of force in violation of this line."

Further Article VI of this agreement provided that

> "both governments agree that their respective heads will meet and in the meantime the representatives of the two sides will meet to discuss the modalities and arrangements for the establishment of durable peace and normalization of relations including the question of repatriation of prisoners of war and civilian internees, a final settlement of Jammu-Kashmir and the resumption of diplomatic relations."

Jana Sangh was very much opposed to the Simla Agreement for two reasons.

One, it nullified the declared policy of India that Kashmir was not the subject of negotiation with any other country and secondly, it made Pakistan a party to the final settlement of Pakistan question.

As Prof Balraj Madhok observed that

> "the Simla agreement not only re-opened the Kashmir question but also it clearly made Pakistan a party to the final settlement of the question. This completely nullified the declared and often-repeated stand of India that Kashmir was not negotiable and that Pakistan had no locus stand in Kashmir."[47]

Prof Madhok deplored that he called "the dismal performance of Indira Gandhi." He called it "a betrayal of the Indian people, armed forces."

References

1. KM Panikkar, *Gulab Singh: The Founder of Kashmir* (London) Martin Hopkinson Ltd. (1930), p 104.
2. See, *The Kashmir Question* (Lucknow: the Research Institute of India, 1950), p 3.
3. HS Gururaj Rao: *Legal Aspects of the Kashmir Problem* (Bombay: Asia Publishing House, 1967), pp 18-19.
4. Quoted by AG Noorani: *The Kashmir Question* (Bombay, Manaktalas 1964), p 21.
5. Quoted by AG Noorani, *op cit*, p 23.
6. *Ibid*.
7. *Ibid*, p 23.
8. Quoted by AG Noorani, *op cit*, p 92.
9. UN Document, S/628, 21, 1948.
10. UN Document, S/646, dated 15, 1948.
11. See the text of the agreement in GS Bhargava, *Successor, Surrender? The Simla Summit* (New Delhi: Sterling Publishers, 1972), p 124.
12. Resolutions on Jammu-Kashmir obsolete India tells UN, *The Indian Express* (New Delhi), Vol XIIV, No 249, 16 October 1976, p 1.

13. *Manifesto and Programme of Bharatiya Jana Sangh* adopted by the Bharatiya Pratinidhi Sabha.
14. *1958 Manifesto*.
15. Syama Prasad Mukherjee: 'Presidential Address', *The Statesman* (New Delhi, 27 October 1951).
16. Prem Nath Dogra: Presidential Address at Jodhpur Session of Bharatiya Jana Sangh on 30 December 1954.
17. Resolution passed at the 8th Annual Session of the Bharatiya Jana Sangh at Nagpur, 23-25 January 1960.
18. Resolution No 3 passed at the 11th Annual Session of the Bharatiya Jana Sangh at Ahmedabad, 28-30 December 1963.
19. *Ibid*.
20. Balraj Madhok: *Selected Speeches in the Lok Sabha* (Delhi, Deepak Publications), p 17.
21. *Organiser* (Editorial) 29 August 195.
22. *Ibid*.
23. The Jammu-Kashmir Praja Parishad which was merged with the Jana Sangh in 1963 advocated the full and unconditional accession of the State of India. The Parishad gave away cry:

    Ek Desh Men Do Vidhan—In one country two constitutions

    Ek Desh Men Do Nishan—In one country two flags.

    Ek Desh Men Do Pradhan—In one country two Prime Ministers

    Nahin chalegi, nahin chalegi—will not be tolerated (English translation)
24. Bachraj Vyas: *Presidential Address at the Bharatiya Pratinidhi Sabha Session*, New Delhi, 17-18 August 1965 (Delhi: Navchetan Press, 1965), p 7.
25. The Gajendragadkar Commission had been constituted by the Jammu-Kashmir State Government to find out the cause of unrest among the people of Jammu-Kashmir. Among other things, the Commission made the following recommendations:

    (i) For the removal of regional imbalances, separate Regional Development Boards should be constituted for Jammu, Kashmir and Ladakh.

(ii) Recruitment rules for all states services should be framed and implemented.

(iii) The State Government should revise the existing list of backward classes and a high powered Committee be set up to draw up a fresh list of backward classes;

(iv) Article 335 of the Indian Constitution should be made applicable to the Jammu and Kashmir state:

(v) A separate University should be set up in Jammu with arrangements for faculty of law. Besides, a new medical College should be opened at Jammu and an Engineering College in course of time.

For details, *see*, AB Vajpayee, Presidential address, Fifteenth All India Session (Bombay: Shree Raj Mundra Press, 1969), pp 18-20.

26. Lok Sabha Debates, Vol 29, November 1961, Cols 2153-58.
27. *Organiser*, Vol XI, No 31, Delhi, 14 April 1958, p 12.
28. A Moin Zaidi: *The Annual Register of Indian Political Parties*, New Delhi, 1977-79) pp 401-402.
29. *Organiser*, Vol XI, No 10, 15 October 1962.
30. Bharatiya Jana Sangh Party Documents, Vol 3, Resolutions on Defence and External Affairs, Central Office, Vithalbhai Patel Bhavan, New Delhi, 1973), p 117.
31. Bharatiya Jana Sangh Party Documents, Vol 3, *op cit*, p 118.
32. Bharatiya Jana Sangh Party Documents, Vol 3, *ibid*.
33. *Organiser*, Vol XIV, No 11, New Delhi, 31 October 1960, p 15.
34. *Organiser*, Vol XIV, No 11, New Delhi, 31 October 1960, p 16.
35. *Organiser*, Vol XIV, No 11, New Delhi, 31 September 1960; p 14.
36. Nehru's Blunders Regarding Kashmir, BJS Party Documents, *op cit*, p 109.
37. *Ibid*.
38. Central Working Committee, 20 April 1957, Jaunpur, BJS Party documents, *op cit*, p 47.
39. Kashmir in UNO Central Working Committee, 24 November 1957, Hyderabad.

40. Balraj Madhok: 'Kashmir Problem', Bharatiya Sahitya Sadan (New Delhi, nd,) p 28.
41. Bishwanath Singh, "Kutch Award—A Study in Indo-Pak Relations", *Indian Journal of Political Science*, Vol XXIX, No 2, April 1968, pp 155-163.
42. Bharatiya Jana Sangh, Party Documents, Vol 3, Resolutions on Defence and External Affairs, Central Office Vithalbhai Patel Bhavan (New Delhi, 1973), p 131.
43. *Ibid.*
44. *Ibid.*
45. Central Working Committee of Bharatiya Jana Sangh, 15 January 1966, Kanpur.
46. Balraj Madhok: *Bungling in Kashmir* (New Delhi, Hind Pocket Books, 1974), p 162.
47. Balraj Madhok: *Ibid*, p 169.

CHAPTER 5

Arab-Israel Conflict

A Brief History

The Arab-Israel Conflict has been proving intractable. It has caused till now four big wars between the Arab States and Israel. This conflict has turned the whole of West Asia into a boiling pot. It has destabilized the political system in the regime and it has forced the Arab States and Israel to fritter their resources from development to defence and war. Because of this the West Asian region has become a cockpit of world politics in which both the supper powers are intensely interested.

Historical Background

For about four centuries before the First World War the Arab world was under the ruthless misrule of the Roman Empire. The tyranny of the Roman Empire stirred the Arab people from their morbid passivity. They began to think in terms of emancipation. They also started to think in terms of Arab national unity. According to George Antonious,

> "The story of Arab national movement opens in Syria in 1947 with the foundation in Beirut of a modest Literary Society under American patronage."[1]

In 1908, there was a revolution in Turkey spearheaded for separation of the Arabs. This laid to a revolt by the Arabs against Turkey during the First World War.

On 14 May 1948, the USA accorded Israel *de facto* recognition and after some days back, the USSR also gave it *de facto* recognition. At this juncture the well armed and trained Arab armies invaded Israel; it was the question of life and death for the newly born Jewish state of Israel, because there was no trained army with Israel.

Arab States maintained 2,50,00,000 number of trained soldiers, on the other hand the Israel have only 6,50,000 soldiers. So the Arab States had thought that their well trained armies would drive the Jews into the sea and their properties would come in the hands of the Arabs.

During the First World War the British announced a policy of granting independence to Arab States in return of Arab support to the British war and against Turkey. In the meanwhile, Britain and France also signed in March 1910 a treaty which was called the Sykes-Picot Agreement for the division of the Turkish Empire in Asia between Britain and France in the eventual defeat of Turkey in the War. This agreement later on was supplemented by another agreement which put Palestine under the British sphere of influence. At this time the British Secretary of State for Foreign Affairs, Mr AJ Balfour wrote a letter to Lord Rothschild in November 1917, committing British support,

> "to the establishment in Palestine of a 'national home for the Jewish people'. This came to be known as the Balfour Declaration. This was the first official British commitment to support the foundation of Israel. The British support to the Zionist cause went only "so far as compatible with the freedom of the existing population both economic and political."[2]

After the First World War the history of political development in most Asia became a story of struggle between Arab nationalism and Zionism. Turkey was defeated during the First

World War and Palestine was placed under the British Mandate. Britain set out to implement the Balfour Declaration effecting the political right of Arabs. There were two main fronts, one the immigration of the Jews in Palestine, and secondly, purchase of land by the Jews there. The Arabs were opposed to both of them. Consequently, the British government appointed a Royal Commission in 1936 which recommended partition of Palestine for the Arabs and the Jews. This further aggravated the conflict between the two nations.

After the World War, British government referred the problem to the UN in 1947.[3]

The General Assembly of the United Nations passed a resolution on 28 November 1947 asking for partition of Palestine and creation of the State of Israel.[4]

This facilitated the establishment of Israel, but it also stated civil war in Palestine between the Arabs and the Jews. While the Jews accepted the UN's partition plan, the Arabs decided to reject and resist it. The British Government decided to terminate its Mandate on Palestine on 14 May 1948. The Jewish National Assembly met on the same day in Tel Aviv and proclaimed the establishment of the Jewish State of Israel within the area earmaked in the UN partition resolution. The New State was recognised within four days by America and the Soviet Union. But the Arabs started to attack the new State because, to the Arabs,

> "Israel was a colonial offshoot of the Western world, imposed on the oriental world by force."[5]

The Arab countries declared their determination to crush the new state. For this the Palestine Arabs with the help of other Arab countries started a series of invasion on Israel.

According to Lie, "the invasion of Palestine by the Arab States was the first armed aggression which had been since the end of War." According to him,

> "the aim was clear, momentous war of extermination which will be spoken in history like the Mongolian massacres and the crusades."[6]

The happening of these days brought Anglo-American relations to the lowest ebb because Britain supported Arab States, while America supported the Jews.[7]

During the second war between Arab and Israel, the Arab States were not ready to accept the existence of Israel.

It was obvious that the attitude of Israel towards Jerusalem was totally against the Conciliation Commission Report. It was said, "Some important Israel leaders who considered the strategic importance of Jerusalem and the economic advantage of internationalization more important than its historical and religious appeal."[8] While the Israeli people were in favour of internationalization only.[9]

In UN General Assembly Israeli representative strongly protested against Conciliation Commission Report in the context of Jerusalem. He remarked that UN should retain only a functional authority for the supervision of the holy places. So UN is only a supervisory committee.

The American, British and French Foreign Ministers met at London to solve the Middle East problem. But it was hard pill to swallow for the Arab leaders as they were humiliated in first war by what they considered a small western enclave. The Arab State did not want to make peace with Israel as technically superior and well produced Jewish goods would dominate their market and thus they would damage their economy.[10]

Dayan said that on 26 February 1956, President Nasser gave order to start campaign against Israel with full intention of the destruction of Israel. In the meanwhile, France and Israel became very cordial due to their own vested interest. France was not in favour of invasion of Egypt unless Britain would give green signal.

> "If it were not for the Anglo-French operation, it is doubtful it Israel would have launched her campaign and if she had its character both military and political, would have been different."[11]

The Government of France wanted to overthrow Nasser as he was secretly working against their North African empire by helping Algerian nationalists.

On 29 October 1956, Israel invaded Egyptian forces in Sinai when France and Britain were given ultimatum to withdraw their armies to ten miles from each side of Canal. Dayan told

> "We are not within the ten miles of the canal and we have neither interest nor plan to come closer to it."

It was obvious that the whole plan was prepared by Britain and France.

During this war Israel captured whole Sinai Peninsula desert but UN Security Council ordered for stoppage of war and withdrawal of forces.

But the Government of Israel announced that unless its grievances were met and guarantee of security was given, Israel would not withdraw. As Prime Minister Ben-Gurion said,

> "I was insistent on my refusal to pull-out completely unless we had adequate safeguards that this territory would not be used by Egypt as a lease for infiltrations attack, and for blockading Israeli shipping through Canal and the Gulf of Aqaba."[12]

After the Second War Middle East become divided into two blocs—Russian and American became protector of Israel and Russia was helping Arab States. France declared that if any invasion were committed on Israel by Arabs from Gaza Patti or blockade of Israeli ship line in Arabia she would help Israel.[13]

President Nasser began to give slogan for Arab unity. Cairo became the centre of all Arab adventurist activities.

In April 1959, Egypt began to start blockade of Suez Canal for Israeli shipping, Israel Government requested UN, but UN could not do anything.

In the meanwhile President of USA said on 8 May 1963,

> "In the event of aggression, whether direct or indirect, we would support appropriate measures in the UN and adopt other courses of action on our own to prevent or put a stop to such aggression."[14]

Meanwhile President Nasser declared that,

> "the Arabs would never accept a political solution of the Palestine problem, they had the manpower to impose different solution."

Arab-Israel conflict had become the international problem. The western powers also had ambition to increase their influence by supplying arms and ammunitions to Israel. On the other hand, Soviet Russia also had to keep the balance and they were competing to do so by supplying arms to Arabs.[15]

The third war broke out on 5 January 1967 when Israeli forces in a sudden attack reached the western bank of the Suez Canal. It was a question of life and death for the Jews as the Arabs could afford to lose war many times and can continue struggle, while for Israel loss of one war means complete destruction forever.[16] When the third war broke out, the most dramatic confrontation took place and the Arab forces were completely humiliated.

On 6 June 1967 the Security Council by passing resolution S/Res/233, ordered for ceasefire to all parties without charging Israel as aggressor.[17]

The war stopped on 10 June 1967. President Sadat of the UAR went to Israel, addressed the Israeli parliament and pleaded for peace.

15 August 1947, India gained its national independence. It followed a foreign policy which is based on non-alignment. When Palestine question was raised in the UN General Assembly in 1947 India's attitude towards Israel had changed and she supported Arabs as well as Israel, because Arabs and Israel both should be equally treated by India. Indian government could not give full diplomatic representation to Israel due to powerful Muslim pressure on the government through its leaders and members of the government, and love for the Muslim brotherhood.[18]

In the meanwhile, India allowed Israel to open trade consulate at Bombay but did not establish consular office in Israel.

Prime Minister Nehru wanted to give Israel due place, but due to pressure of Muslim minority in India he could not do so, Pandit Nehru told in a discussion with Brig Y Allan of Israel,

> "we regret that because of unfortunate coincidences in the past, normal relation had not been established between India and Israel."

Israel should not interpret this as hostile attitude and he wished Israel 'Prosperity and development'. Brig Y Allan answered that,

> "Mr Nehru hoped that one day normal relations would be established between the two countries."[19]

But this hope is yet to be realized.

For peace in West Asia—for stable peace in West Asia it is essential that:

(1) The Arab countries must relinquish all intentions to annihilate Israel, acknowledge its existence, and develop mutual relation on the basis of peaceful co-operative coexistence.

(2) Israel also must realize that it is basically an Afro-Asian State, and so instead of allowing itself to be used just as an instrument of Western diplomacy in West Asia, should play a respectable and purposeful role. With its economic prosperity and scientific and technological advancement, it can very well become a great source of strength for developing countries of Asia and Africa. But for this, it will have to re-orientate its attitude, cease looking westwards, and develop altogether a new personality.

(3) Israel must co-operate on a large scale for the resettlement of Arab refugees uprooted as a result of the establishment of Israel. The miserable plight of the refugees is a permanent cause for the tension and bitterness subsisting between the Arab and Jews, and it has to be remedied.

(4) The Suez Canal and the Gulf of Aquila must be made open for ships of all nations. The UAR will have the right of a tool from the unilaterally, Similar other sea-routes in other parts of the world should be internationalized.

(5) Israel should withdraw its forces from areas it has occupied in recent conflict.

Jana Sangh demands that the Government of India must revise its West Asia policy with a view to winning the friendship of both, the Arabs and Israelites and creating stable peace in the region. In this context the Jana Sangh wishes to reiterate its demand that the Government of India must take steps to establish full fledged diplomatic relations with Israel.[20]

The Arabs are victims of international politics. Before the Second World War they were tossed about by Britain and France. After the War they have become the plaything of the 'Super powers', America and Russia.

These powers, who have for over 200 years held the developing the underdeveloped nations in political, economic and spiritual thralldom are today exploiting the emotions of the Arabs without bringing any equitable, meaningful solution to their grievances.

Today, many Arab lands have rivers of liquid 'black gold' following under their age-old desert sands. That has of course brought blessings as well as dangers that sudden prosperity always does. For one thing, they are a wasting asset; for another, alternate energy source might be found, and the present bonanza may become obsolete and valueless. Therefore, it is wise to act with foresight when there are resources to plan their future with care.

They are of course, agitated about the rise of Israel as a new power in their midst, like a Jinn in the manner of the tale in the Arabian Nights. But the point to consider dispassionately is whether the Israelis are an alien people who have intruded to exploit the Arabs.

The Arab's own history tells that they are blood brothers of the Israelis and that their religions, customs and manners are extensions of each other's. They are in fact of one race and of one family through the Patriarch Abraham. So why should they listen to the Americans or Russians, to the British or French or Germans who pour poison into their ears?

They should also remember that they as well as the Israelis are Asians like the Iranians. Afghans, Indians, Indonesians, Malaysians and the rest of the people of Asia. They should evolve, and India is interested in evolving an Asian policy, a fruitful policy and that policy must firmly lead to the objective Asians must not kill Asians.

Why can't the problems of the Arabs and Israelis be solved peacefully without killing? And without wasting the fruits of their labour and their fortunes?

Most thinking Arabians have come to realize that Israelis as a viable power in the ancient desert have come to stay. They cannot be and need not be destroyed. Even the Egyptians who out number the Israelis in sixteen to one ratio, have accepted that fact.

But there are ugly and irritating elements in the situations. The lost lands are one, and the self-exiled Palestinians are the other. The lost lands concern mostly the Egyptians, and Palestinians deserve not merely lip sympathy but a constructive policy to restore them to their homes and to rehabilitate them to live peaceful and fruitful lives. This can be done, and it is in the realm of practical realization.

The sensitive in the Arab-Israel conflict are Jordan, Lebanon and Israel, the others are peripheral. Any constructive and enduring solutions must concentrate on these constituents of the conflict

All the people in the States of Jordan, Lebanon and Israel are racially one people—Semites. They have as Muslims, Christians and Jews, a common cultural heritage in the Bible.

Here is where Indian statesmanship has a great opportunity to serve the best interest of our Arab and Israeli friends. At first both may react with scepticism, for both are emotionally unbalanced. They are bound to accept this Indian proposal which is far superior to any that Western powers may propose at Geneva or the United Nations may concoct at New York. They will be concerned more with exploiting both together as one people.

Asian conflicts and misunderstanding must be settled on Asian soil, and by Asians themselves. That is a sound doctrine.

The Jana Sangh has formulated a proposal as follows for the solution of the Arab-Israel conflict.

Basic Middle-East Data—1965

Country	*Capital*	*Area*	*Population*
Israel	Jerusalem	7,993	23,38,300
Egypt	Cairo	3,86,198	2,65,93,000
Syria	Damascus	72,234	50,67,000
Iraq	Baghdad	1,72,000	72,63,000
Jordan	Amman	37,500	16,80,000
Saudi Arabia	Ryadh	8,70,000	80,00,000
Kuwait	Kuwaiti City	5,800	3,22,000
Lebanon	Beirut	4,000	18,22,000
Sudan	Khartoum	9,67,500	1,24,70,000
Algeria	Algiers	1,13,883	1,10,20,000
Tunisia	Tunis	58,000	42,54,000
Yemen	Sana	75,000	5,000,000
Morocco	Rabat	1,72,104	11,925,000

Attitude of Jana Sangh Towards Arab-Israel Conflict

The attitude of Jana Sangh towards the Arab-Israel conflict has been one the critical to India's policy because Indian government in view of the Jana Sangh was following a blatantly pro-Arab and anti-Israel policy. Such a policy, Jana Sangh leaders said was not warranted by the attitude of Israel and Arab States towards India on some of the major issues confronting India's foreign policy.

Jana Sangh leaders said Arab States adopted a hostile attitude towards India in all major conflicts of this country with Pakistan whereas Israel has consistently been pro-India in its stand at the United Nations. The Jana Sangh leaders said that the India's pro-Arab and anti-Israel policy was faulty on two grounds, first, it was illogical and against India's interest and sense of self-respect. Secondly, it caused to have India's professions of non-alignment.

India's policy has also been incongruous. As Prof Madhok said,

> "it suffers from glaring incongruities, while recognition has been given to the Communist government of China on the ground that it is the government which the Chinese people have accepted and which is now well-entrenched in power, the same has been refused to Israel which is even more firmly established reality."

The BJS has been passing resolutions at its various sessions advocating establishment of diplomatic relations with Israel. The Jana Sangh has been advocating this line of policy for various reasons.[21] Israel is regarded as the only real democracy in West Asia. By establishing relations with Israel, India would provide support to democracy and would also improve its relations with a number of African States. Further, India would also promote political stability in West Asia by acting as a bridge of negotiations between Israel and Arab States. This will also be in the self-respect of this vast country. The Jana Sangh is thinking that India's present policy of blatant partnership is due to the UAR whose policy according to *Organiser* is "Love me have enemy."[22]

What the Jana Sangh was advocating was a plea for neither being pro-Arab nor pro-Israel but deciding issue on merits. While it accepted Israel's right to exist, and consequently rejected Arab clamouring to annihilate Israel, at the same time it deplored Israel's tendency to occupy and grab Arab territory. The Jana Sangh also, support the plea to resettle the Palestine refugees. Thus on June 1967, the Jana Sangh Working Committee at its meeting at Simla said,

> "For stable peace in West Asia it is essential that this policy does not appear to be unduly in favour of any party in the case. It is only pro-reason."

Earlier in January 1965, the Jana Sangh Working Committee had said:

> "Israel is the only real democracy in the West Asia. It is a highly developed country and has been playing an increasingly important role in the economic development of newly emerging African countries with which she has developed very good relations by contributing to stability in West Asia but will also improve her position in number of African states. It is therefore, imperative that India must have full diplomatic relations with Israel."[23]

The Jana Sangh's support for establishment of diplomatic relations with Israel is based on several considerations.

Israel has come to stay; secondly, it would mean termination of insult to the world Jewry.

Thirdly, it would project an image of Indian impartiality and independence in the world and particularly in West Asia.

Fourthly, it would hold India to pay its establishing and mediatory role in that reason.

In Jana Sangh's view, the policy of India although has been unduly pro-Arab and it gives the impression of being dictated by the Arab countries. India's independent attitude would also have the sixth consequence that is, forcing the Arab countries to shed their anti-India bias.

Thus, Prof Madhok said that out of 13 Arab countries, 12 countries have adopted an attitude verging on enmity with India. Only the UAR has been partially neutral. He said that if the UAR can be friend of India as well as India's enemy like China and Pakistan, there is no reason why India cannot be friendly with both UAR and Israel. Prof Madhok said that looking at the problem from the point of view of idealism or pure realism, India should have the closest relations with Israel.[24]

This view was also supported by Deendayal Upadhyaya in his presidential address at the Calicut session of the party in December 1967.

Jana Sangh felt that India's policy of support to the Arab was against its profession of secularism at home. Because the country was supporting the forces of religious fanaticism represented by the Arab obscurant led by Saudi Arabia and Jordan.

Jana Sangh feels that India should seize the opportunity to be friendly to the world Jewry by normalising relations with Israel because as the *Organiser* wrote,

> "Israel is the hope of all the Jews the world over; and it is the symbol of stability in a very unstable part of the world."

The *Organiser* said that establishment of diplomatic relations with Israel would

> "at once convince the world that we do understand the realities of the world situation; that we can see which side of our bread is buttered."[25]

According to the Party journal *Organiser*,

> "the Arabs want to simply throw off Israelis into the sea and this is nothing but a pale reproduction of the Nazi animus, quite unworthy of peaceable mankind."[26]

The Party believes that

> "Indian can checkmate Pakistani influence in the Middle East by normalizing its relations with Israel. The Jana Sangh does not suggest for a moment that India should be

> in anyway less friendly to the Arab countries. But it does not see any reason why India should side with them against Israel, when they (Arab countries) don't side with us against Pakistan."[27]

Delivering speech Balraj Madhok said,

> "In West Asia, India has been trying all the time to be with the Arab countries. We have given them all our support on all issues. But what has been their response? When the Chinese invaded India, UAR could not make up its mind whether India was the aggressor or China? Again when Pakistan invaded, they met at Casablanca and passed a resolution in favour of Pakistan. Out of 13 Arab countries, 12 are virtually inimical towards India and only one country, UAR, is partially neutral."

On the other hand, the Jana Sangh laments, we have been opposing Israel, which is the strongest and the only democratic country in West Asia and which can be of so much help to us in that region. This attitude must change. We must deal with every Arab country individually. Jordan and Saudi Arabia have been, all the time, helping Pakistan who is our enemy. We should treat them as our enemies. We must have closest relations with Israel. There is no reason why UAR should complain about it. When the UAR can say that she was good friend of India and also a good friend of Pakistan and Communist China, why can't India tell that we are a good friend of UAR, but at the same time we want to be a good friend of Israel also which is as good a member of UN as UAR. The argument about India losing Arab votes in the United Nations is considered as fallacious by the Jana Sangh. In the first place, according to it, there is no surety of Arab votes where our interests are involved. Secondly, if we change our attitude and be friend to Israel we might be able to create public opinion in so many other countries in our favour. It is the Jews who influence the public opinion in America and France more than anybody else. Besides, Israel has very good relations with many African countries as well.

Therefore, whether we look at from idealist point of view or whether we look at it on purely realistic and national interest's point of view, Jana Sangh sees no reason why we should not have the closest relations with Israel.[28] Deendayal Upadhyaya also held the same view.[29]

The Bharatiya Jana Sangh believes that India should enhance its peace-keeping influence in this area and religious fanaticism and hegemonistic ambitions should be discouraged by the international community. It advocated that the

> "interest of different ethnic and political entities with the Greeks, Turks, Jews, Christians, Druges and others."[30]

The *Organiser* further writes that it was the Israeli which enabled India to be a member of United Nations Security Council on 20 November 1966, while the Arab League to whom India alone in the world recognition, acted against India there. The party learnt that despite all these Israeli overtures, India is not recognizing Israel as an independent nation.[31]

The *Organiser* editorial said that the funny part of this affair was that while a majority of Arab States show loyalty for Pakistan, but to please them Indian government is displeasing Israel. When Pakistan attacked India in 1965, the Jordanian representative took anti-Indian attitude in the United Nations Security Council. On the other hand, when Israel took retaliatory raid in Jordan, Indian government condemned Israel. The cruelty of the joke was that on the very day of that condemnation, November 17, the king of Jordan signed a communique with the President of Pakistan supporting the Pakistan claim over Kashmir.[32]

Prof ML Sondhi, Bharatiya Jana Sangh MP described Congress India as 'the fourteenth Arab State'.[33] According to him, not having diplomatic relations with Israel is wholly unrealistic policy of Government of India. Neither it is fair to Israel nor even to the Arab States. India should help in the dialogue between the belligerent for amity, and India's economy is linked with both Israel and the Arab States. India has a greater role in keeping peace in West Asia and to safeguard the national interests. The dramatic failure of Arab monolithism underlines the importance of recognizing that a small state like Israel is fact of significance which we can ignore only at our peril.[34]

In a letter, Prof Michael Brecher, Professor of Political Science, McGill University Montreal (Canada) asked,

> "How far India has fallen from these values (non-alignment, impartiality, pragmatic idealism for the new nations) and standards of behaviour. Her words and deeds during the Middle East crisis of the last fortnight have saddened friends of India every where. She has proclaimed a one-sided and uncritical policy in support of the Arab dictatorship, progressive and otherwise in their efforts to strangle the only truly democratic West Asian state Indian leaders have swallowed and repeat parrot like the Arab-created and Soviet fostered charge about Israel's alleged help from imperialism.
>
> Does India now believe in the murder of small states? Does India no longer believe in the equality of all nations in the Principles of non-interference, mutual respect, freedom of navigation in international waterways and in the host of other guides to civilized behaviour laid down by her statesman in the past? One is reluctantly led to ask whether India ever did believe these principles.
>
> Had such a biased pro-Arab policy been successful in the past, it might have been possible to excuse, or at least

> to understand, the Government of India's painfully immoral posture. The fact is, however, that this policy has consistently failed to win Arab support in India's time of need; the violation of self proclaimed principle has ill-served India's national interests.
>
> It is not too late for India to return to the path of moral courage, genuine, non-alignment, and support for democracy in that troubled area of conflict."[35]

The Central Working Committee of Bharatiya Jana Sangh objects to the partisan policy pursued by the Government of India with regard to the recent Arab-Israel war. Although India should have exercised its influence first to check any eruption of hostilities between the Arabs and Israelis and after war had broken out with a view to restore peace. Instead of doing this, the Government of India has, right from the outset, extended its blind support to the Arabs. As a result, its policy has neither promoted the cause of peace nor served India's own wider interests.

It is obvious that the part played by the big powers in the West Asia struggle should be an eye-opener for the smaller and developing countries. Soviet Russia had a hand in the establishment of Israel and so it does not lie in her mouth to describe that state as the product of Anglo-American diplomacy. Today, in pursuance of its global objective Russia has been busy fanning Arab fanaticism. The United States and Britain, keen to retain their grip on this strategically valuable Oil-belt have been on the one hand encouraging formation of an Islamic bloc and propping up reactionary regimes like those of Jordan and Saudi Arabia while on the other they have been fast arming Israel with a view to using it as an effective power for the furtherance of their designs. It is necessary that all the countries of West Asia understand the strategy of the big powers, and instead of acting as their puppets strive to settle their dispute mutually on the basis of peace and co-existence.[36]

Thus Bharatiya Jana Sangh demands that the Government of India must raise its West Asia policy with a view to winning the friendship, of both the Arabs and Israelis and creating stable peace in the region. In this context the Jana Sangh wishes to reiterate its demand that the Government of India must take steps to establish full-fledged diplomatic relations with Israel.

Jana Sangh objects that the all-out support extended by India to Arabs cannot be justified either on the ground of reciprocity or of national interests. Similarly the illogical stand India has taken in regard to Taiwan, which happens to be our most important window on and the most determined foe of China, not only runs counter to India's interests out also makes a mockery of India's Arab-Israel policy.

India's policy towards Arab States needs to be reviewed in the light of attitude adopted by them towards India during the Bangladesh crisis. If the Arab countries can be friendly with India and Pakistan simultaneously why cannot India also have friendly relations with both the Arab as well as Israel? India has accorded recognition to Israel but has not as yet established full-fledged diplomatic ties with it. If the Arab countries take side with Pakistan only because Pakistan is a Muslim country, then India too needs to tell these Arab-friends that India's friendship cannot be taken for granted. The Arab countries must realize that when they can have warm relations with India's enemies there is no reason why India should not have relations with Israel.

At Poona Central Working Committee's meeting, the Bharatiya Jana Sangh passed a resolution on 6th October 1956 and urged upon the Government of India

> "to ensure, in the interest of all concerned, that freedom of navigation through the Suez Canal be guaranteed by an international agency. The Working Committee, therefore, urged upon the Government of India to exert its influence for securing an international guarantee of free navigation for ships of all countries at all times through the Canal. The Committee felt that such a guarantee was not incompatible with the sovereignty of Egypt over the Suez."[37]

But the Party was against what it called the double standards of Indian foreign policy which applied to Hungary and Suez Canal issues. While Government of India opposed and condemned British, French and Israeli action against Egypt but when the case of Hungry was brought in the UN General Assembly, India voted against the resolution urging the withdrawal of Russian troops from Hungary and suggesting holding of free elections under UN auspices. In this way in view of the Sangh, India supported one aggressor (Russia) and condemned the other aggressor.[38] The Party, however, did not condemn the Israeli action. Sangh condemned Israeli attack on Egypt too in unequivocal terms.

The Sangh considered the claim of Egypt of Its sovereignty over Suez Canal which passes through Egypt as justified and deserving of support, but at the same time the fact could not be ignored that Suez is the most important International Highway in the world as it provides the shortest sea-link between Asia and Europe and as such not only trade and commerce, but also normal cultural and social intercourse in between Europe, Asia and Australia depend very much upon free and unrestricted navigation through this Canal.[39]

The Working Committee of Bharatiya Jana Sangh urged upon the Government of India to exert its influence for securing an international guarantee of free navigation for ships of all countries at all times through the Canal. The Jana Sangh felt that such a guarantee is not incompatible with the sovereignty of Egypt over the Suez.[40]

Jana Sangh remarked that free passage through the canal is necessary for all countries without exception in the matter of the Suez Canal. So freedom of traffic along the Suez Canal must be assured without delay by an international agreement.

The Bharatiya Jana Sangh bitterly condemned the aggression of the Anglo-French power in Egypt, though they might have acted under great provocation because of President Nasser's unilateral repudiation of an International Agreement. The Anglo-French power had however, somewhat redeemed their conduct by yielding to the directive of UNO and withdrawing their forces.[41]

Jana Sangh equally condemned the Russian intervention in Hungary and the brutalities committed there against Hungarians struggling for national Independence and further condemned the Russian refusal to abide by the directive of UNO to withdraw her forces from Hungry and even to admit the UN observers there.[42]

Jana Sangh observed that the domination of the nation by another under any pretext whatsoever was wrong and felt that such attempted domination from whichever quarter it may come should be opposed stoutly.

Jana Sangh felt that the policy of appeasement is all round dangerous to the security and derogatory to the honour of India. It must be abandoned immediately and a stern and realistic policy must be followed to uphold India's honour and dignity and defend her territory.

Therefore, India's interest in peace in West Asia and re-opening of Suez Canal was more immediate and pressing than many other countries. India, therefore, must play the role of a mediator and peace-maker between Arabs and Israel instead of taking sides with any of them. The present policy of touch-me-not towards Israel is not rational. It is a partisan policy with communal motivations and overtones. It must be changed and steps must be taken to normalize relations with Israel.[43]

The third Arab-Israel war broke out when Egypt proceeded to block the passage of Israeli ships through the Suez Canal and the Gulf of Aqaba.

The Egyptian argument that it is fully within its rights in keeping Israeli ships and all other ships carrying strategic goods to the Israeli port of Eilat—out of the Gulf of Aqaba, is not very reasonable. The Gulf of Aqaba is common to four countries—Egypt, Israel, Jordan and Saudi Arabia, and makes the Gulf, even though very narrow, international waters. Today Egypt is blocking the Israeli port of Eilat, tomorrow it could block the Jordanian port of Aqaba.

The convention on the 'Territorial Sea and Contiguous Zone', adopted by the United Nations Conference on the Law of the Sea, 27 April 1958, by 62 votes to 1 with 9 abstentions and effective as from 10 September 1964, says in its clause 4:

> "There shall be no suspension of the innocent passage of foreign ships through straits which are used for international navigation between one part of the high sea and another part of the high sea or the territorial sea of a foreign state."

Israel is surrounded on all sides by hostile Arab countries. Its 27 lakh population will have to face more than 10 crore Arabs. Before the fighting broke out, 80,000 Egyptians were facing 30,000 Israelis on the Sinai front. Forty thousand Syrians and 40,000 Jordanians were menacing Israel in the North and the East. Saudi Arabia had sent 20,000 soldiers to fight Israel on the Jordan frontier. Five thousand Palestine Liberation Army men threatened in the Gaza strip. Five thousand Iraqis—who don't have Sudan—also started moving troops into Egypt to fight Israel. And all over the Middle East, Mullahs were shrieking to Friday congregations 'in the name of Allah' to prepare for 'Jihad' and 'wipe Israel off the map'. Israel could not be expected to shut its eyes and then complain, India-like, of being 'surprised' and 'stabbed in the back'.

In the first twenty-four hours of fighting, Israel captured the Jordanian section of the prestigious city of Jerusalem and the Egyptian town of Gaza. The claims of aeroplanes shot down by the two sides were so contradictory that they can't be believed. But the Israeli Air Force seemed to have the upper hand-at least for the present. What is the military strength of the two sides and how is fighting likely to go if it goes on for some time? [44]

One cannot forecast more about the conclusion of war than one can foretell the result of a cricket match.

But it can be said with reasonable certainty that the fighting will not be allowed to go on for very long. Such lengthening of war would endanger oil interests. It will also threaten a nuclear holocaust, which nobody wants. Fighting will continue till one or the other side gets a good knock and is sober enough to compromise. At that stage the Big Powers will intervene and stop the fighting. If Israel does better than the Arabs, Russia will insist on withdrawal to old line; if it's the other way around, that demand will come from USA.[45]

MC Chhagla, India's Minister for External Affairs said in the UN that the creation of Israel had increased the tension in West Asia. This was criticized by several Jana Sangh leaders. Atal Bihari Vajpayee objected to this statement and asked the Foreign Minister as to what was the meaning of his opinion that "the creation of Israel has given rise to tension between Israel and the Arab countries." He also criticized Chhagla's suppressing attitude towards Israel.

Chhagla replied that existence of Israel was a fact of life and also it was a fact that the creation of that state had led to tension between Arab and Israel. So Israel was fully responsible to create the trouble.

But Madhu Limaye (SSP) condemned the government's statement and mentioned that one or two things mentioned in the Minister's statement sounded rather unilateral in the assertion of India's friendship with the UAR, which was never unilateral.

When India was invaded by China (1962) and Pakistan (1965) the UAR did not side with India. The Arab nations fully supported Pakistan and China.

Prof Sondhi asked, if the government would be prepared to take steps to recognize Israel on the condition that Israel established an independent personality free from American control. Chhagla said India had recognized Israel but had no diplomatic relations with her.[46]

The Prime Minister Indira Gandhi criticized Israel for having escalated the situation in to an armed conflict. She said this war is likely to expand in to a much wider one, drawing into its vortex other countries and developing perhaps into a world war.[47] This idea had been fully supported by the communist party. But the opposition parties like the Jana Sangh, Swatantra and SSP bitterly criticized the statement which had been given by Prime Minister Indira Gandhi.

Opposition leaders like Prof NG Ranga, Atal Bihari Vajpayee (JS), SN Dwivedy (PSP), Dr Lohia (SSP), Acharya Kripalani (Ind) blamed that without any reliable evidence Indira Gandhi blamed Israel.

Atal Bihari Vajpayee declared that while India valued the friendship of the Arabs, 'extermination of Israel' was not acceptable. This brought forth an assurance from Indira

Gandhi that India would not be a party to the destruction of any country.[48]

According to Jana Sangh there is no doubt that refugee problem is human problem. But it has made more tragedy by the behaviour of the Arab States who made the Arab refugees their pawn for their political game and to divert the attention of the jury of their people at home. Still the refugees are living on UN charity, staying in dirty tents or in sheds while the Arab nations are getting richer. Instead of solving the Palestinian refugee problem they are using them for their political game.[49]

The *Organiser* further said that

> "had the Palestine Arabs foreseen all this before they would have probably made their peace with the Palestine Jews and never joined hands with other Arabs to disintegrated Palestine."[50]

Furthermore, the Jana Sangh charged on Government of India that

> "Fools rush in where angels fear to tread and Government of India's position in the present crisis is no doubt the same. When there is confusion about the point that who fired the first shot on 6 June 1967 war—Egypt or Israel—the Government of India was charging Israel of Muslim appeasement to international levels."[51]

With respect to Al-Aqsa Mosque issue and vis-a-vis Government of India's foreign policy, the Bharatiya Jana Sangh was very much critical about the statement of Dinesh Singh, Foreign Minister of India. It is said that the Hitlerian anti-Jew stance of Indian Foreign Minister is inexplicable, even Russia, Arabs, and Muslim world's latest friend (China) refused to blame Israel for the crime of an individual, while USA, and Russia were playing to cool down the West-Asian crisis from an explosion. Dinesh Singh however, rushed in where United

States and USSR feared to tread.[52] It raised several pertinent questions:

(i) If Israel could not be absolved to responsibility for the fire just because Jerusalem was in Israel, will India be held responsible for the theft of the Prophet's hair in Srinagar some years ago?[53]

(ii) In June 1967 Muslims in Srinagar burnt to ashes two churches of the Christians just because the Israel defeated the Arabs thousands of miles away. Is India to be blamed for this sacrilege against the Christian world?

(iii) In 1965, Pakistani pilots destroyed a church in Ambala. Shall we, according to the queer logic of Government of India, allow the Christians to blame us? Can we absolve of responsibility for failing to protect the churches?

(iv) The Al-Aqsa mosque was destroyed by earthquakes thrice in its 1,300 years of existence. Will Government of India say Israelis cannot be absolved of responsibility for this act of God because they believed in God?

(v) While Jerusalem was under the occupation of Jordan, a Muslim country, there were two fires in the same mosque one in 1949 and another in 1964. Will Government of India hold the Muslim government of Jordan responsible of the fires.[54]

The *Organiser*, wrote that

> "One have hoped for counsels of moderation of restraint from a government so thoroughly familiar with the civil and dangers of religious hostility, communal strife and violence in pursuit of political ends.[55]

The Jana Sangh paper further added that,

> "violence partisan pro-Muslim stance of Government of India was however, creating a new international monster—Muslimism, that spell danger to the integrity of nations. It was, therefore, awfully unreasonable, utterly opportunistic, communal and reactionary against the Government of India to poke its secular nose in Al-Aqsa. India was neither an Islamic country nor an Arab country to get excited over the matter beyond the universal human right of freedom of religion. India burnt its fingers in the folly that was what Khilafat movement. It had no intention of having anything to do with what threatens to develop into Khilafat movement number 2."[56]

While Indian government welcomed the terrorist Al-Fateh in India, the same group was in Pakistan saying that "help Kashmir Muslims in their Jihad against Kafirs."

The *Organiser* wrote that India was promoting a private undeclared war against Israel. Jana Sangh was highly critical of the Rabat Affairs. It said that Soviet Russia and China have large Muslim population but they did not participate in this religious summit. Why Indian government insisted to participate in this conference? In this way it was dividing the country once again on religious lines and reducing Hindus to the status of less favoured citizens called non-Hindus.[57] In this connection, a leading Nepali newspaper *Commoner* asked,

> "what has been surprising is that India insisted on attending this conference at all. She never calls a Hindu Conference."

The last year when the world religious conference wanted India, the home of the ancient religions of the world, to send a delegation, the External Affairs Ministry sent a curt 'no' saying we are not a Hindu State. Nepalese think that Government of India insulted the King and stopped him from addressing an RSS rally in Nagpur on the ground that it would promote communalism, but it thinks nothing of whipping Muslim fanaticism.[58]

The Editorial of the *Organiser* asked whether India wants to join Muslim International, which was planning to defend Islam against all its enemies. The All India Arab Association from its Headquarters at Hyderabad said,

> "If the Participants of the Islamic Summit really wish to defeat Israel and save Islam, then they should revive the institution of Khilafat. This is the only effective measure to meet all the enemies of Islam."

The *Organiser* asked whether Indira Gandhi wanted to start a second Khilafat Movement to liquidate all 'infidels' like Israelis and Hindus.

Secondly, the Muslim countries of the world now want to organize a Muslim Secretariat stationed in Rabat which according to the King Hassan of Morocco was 'the capital of Islam'. The *Organiser* asked whether India will be represented in it? Would India be ruled from New Delhi or from this new Caliphate capital? Should our Jawans be sent to fight the enemies of Islam?[59] According to Prof ML Sondhi, Jana Sangh MP, the unanimous invitation had a certain style, the result of Pakistan's strategy to malign India.[60] The more the government does about Rabat, the more fool it makes of itself. The Sangh was surprised to hear Foreign Minister, saying that the imperialists were responsible for what happened at Rabat. When we knew that the imperialists were going to insult us there, why did we go there? And why don't we regret having gone there? There is no doubt as far as our pro-Muslim and anti-Israel Middle East policy would run, how can we understand the values of our announced principles.[61] It said that India's Foreign Ministry had taken a wisest fool's step with respect to Rabat.[62] According to Jana Sangh party, the role played by President Nasser in the whole episode was blatantly opportunistic. It was he who persuaded India to come into the meeting so that they may be able to prevail over the reactionary elements of the Summit. But due to the economic obligations from reactionary governments like those of Saudi Arabia, Egypt could not openly oppose them. So during India's trouble it remained silent. Further, it was at the direction of UAR that the term, 'the representatives of Indian Muslims' was included among the participants of the conference. Paradoxically enough, it thought, it was thereby doing India a good turn.[63]

Atal Bihari Vajpayee, giving presidential address in Patna at the sixteenth All India Session of the Bharatiya Jana Sangh, said on 28, 30 December 1969,

> "India's experience at Rabat and the attitude taken up by various participating countries towards us should compel rethinking about the Government of India's West Asia policy. This policy had proved utterly barren, neither had it promoted India's own interest nor had it contributed anything towards bringing about peace in the region. While there should be no weakening of our centuries-old ties with the Arab countries, our policy of treating Israel as an untouchable must be completely abandoned. Along with Britain and America, Soviet Russia also was a party to the formation of Israel. The Arab countries must accept Israel's existence and negotiate with it for the establishment of stable peace in the area. Israel should vacate the Arab territories it has occupied."[64]

While supporting India in its demand for the vacation of Indian territory seized by Pakistan and Communist China, Atal Bihari Vajpayee said, "Friendship cannot be a one way traffic."

Over Bangladesh issue, the Bharatiya Jana Sangh was highly critical of pro-Pakistani policy of all the Muslim countries of West-Asia and Africa. It demanded that the Government of

India must revise its barren West-Asia policy as our late Prime Minister Lal Bahadur Shastri had done without hearing for the resentment of the Arab country and visited Israeli trade pavilion in Ahmedabad fair.[65]

Thus, all opposition parties criticized the pro-Arab policy of government. According to Atal Bihari Vajpayee the Rabat Conference was the summit of Islamic country. So it is highly objectionable for India to attend that conference. Surendra Nath Dwivedi said,

> "this is a national humiliation. After 1962 NEFA debacle I think, there is no parallel to the humiliation that we have received now."[66]

Atal Bihari Vajpayee told that it was a communal approach.

Bhai Mahavir, a prominent leader of Jana Sangh, said that Indian government was not invited in Rabat conference, only Indian Muslim community was invited. Dinesh Singh told some members of Parliament that this decision of participating into the conference was taken at the request of certain Muslim members of cabinet and certain Muslim organizations of the country. So it was not the decision of government actually but it was compelled to take this decision. Therefore, this policy was totally against the secular policy of India.

Jana Sangh thinks that Israel has, as such, right to exist as the vast and numerous Arab States. In any case, Israel occupies only a small portion of the vast stretch of Arab land extending from the Atlantic coast of North Africa up to the Persian Gulf. This is evident from a comparative study of the area and population of the different countries in the region.

References

1. George Antonious: *Arab Awakening* (New York, JB Lippincott Company, 1939), p 13.

2. James Pakes: *A History of Palestine* (New York, Oxford University Press 1949), p 287.
3. Survey, 1845-50., *op cit*, p 237.
4. Resolution No 181 (II). *See also* UN Year Book 1947-48.
5. Maximum Robision: *Israel and Arabs* (Penguin Books, 1968), p 45.
6. Trygve Lie: *In the Cause of Peace* (New York, MacMillan Co, 1954), p 174.
7. Kirk: Survey, *op cit*, p 273.
8. Edi, Robinson D: *Under Rife* (New York, WW Nortan and Co, 1968), p 16. "The Arab must unite their efforts and prepare their weapons for the next round...," said PM Fares el-Khoury of Syria.
9. MC Donald: *My Mission in Israel*, *op cit*, p 189.
10. M Lonides: *Divide and Lose*: *The Arab Revolt 1955 to 58* (London, Geoffray Bhs 1960), p 79, both ways. It was morally wicked of writers, "They were attacked, and they fought to prevent the Zionists from enjoying what was theirs. But they were incompetent to fight, and thus, failed. As aggressors they had no right to win, for their military incompetence they deserved to lose. They should have been loyal to the United Nations' decision to consequences of defeat for victory goes to those who are strong. The Jews were right. Anyway they had beaten the Arabs in the war. It was right for the Jews to fight to acquire and wrong for the Arabs to fight to hold."
11. Thomas Huge: *The Suez Affair* (Middlesex, Weidenfield and Nicoloson, 1967, p 92.
12. Kissing's Archives, p 15, 86, 15201, 15205.
13. Home, CD: *The Arabs and Israel* (London, the Bodley Head, 1968, p 34.
14. Current Notes on International Affairs, Israel Recent Development Departnment of External Affairs (Canberra, Australia) Vol 34, No 6 (June 1963), p 15
15. RS and WS Churchill: *The Six days World* (London, Heinemann 1967), p 23.
16 Aharon Cohe: *Israel and the Arab World* (London, WH, 1970), p 533. "Israel with four out off every five man in her army, a civilian could not

afford to maintain her forces mobilised indefinitely, people were eager to fight." RS and WS Churchill, *op cit*, pp 53-54.

17. UN Chronicle: *op cit*, 10 July 1967, at the 6 June meeting.
18. Maulana Azad was a reputed Congressman and a powerful member of Nehru Cabinet; he did not like that India having diplomatic relations with Israel. So every move of Nehru for diplomatic relations with Israel was blocked by him on the threat of alienation of Muslim votes.
19. *Asian Recorder*, 1959, p 2394.
20. Central Working Committee of Bharatiya Jana Sangh, Simla, 30 June 1967.
21. *Organiser*, Vol VII, No 21, 4 January 1954.
22. *Organiser*, Editorial, Vol 18, No 33, 29 March 1965.
23. 12th Party Session, Vijayawada, 1965.
24. Madhok: *What Bharatiya Jana Sangh Shares For*, Ahmedabad Junior Chamber of Commerce, 1966.
25. *Organiser*, 3 April 1966.
26. "Why must India blindly Follow the Arab in Their War on Jews" Editorial, *Organiser*, Vol 18, No 33 (29 March 1965).
27. *Ibid* (5 Sept., 1965), p 3.
28. "What BJS Stands for", *op cit*, p 1.
29. See Deendayal Upadhyaya, Presidential Address, fourteenth Annual Session, Calicut, December 1967, p 23.
30. Manifestoes and Party Publications Jana Sangh, 1968, pp 51-52
31. "Those funny chaps of the Foreign ministry" (Editorial) *Organiser*, Vol XX, No 16 (27 November 1966).
32. *Ibid*.
33. *Ibid*, p 7.
34. *Ibid*.
35. *Organiser*, Vol XX, No 45, p 2.
36. Arab-Israel War, Bharatiya Jana Sangh Party Documents, Vol 3. Resolutions on Defence and External Affairs, Central Office Vithalbhai Patel Bhavan, New Delhi, 1973, p 137.

37. Bharatiya Jana Sangh, Party Documents, Vol 3 (Resolutions on Defence and External Affairs), Central Office, Vithalbhai Patel Bhavan, New Delhi (India), July 1973, p 45.
38. Editorial, *Organiser*, Vol X, No 13, 19 November 1956, p 1.
39. "SUEZ CRISIS", Bharatiya Jana Sangh (Party Documents, Central Office Vol 3. New Delhi, 1973), p 44.
40. "Navigation in Suez", Central Working Committee, Poona, 6 October 1956.
41. "HUNGARIAN AND SUEZ CRISIS", The All India Session of Bharatiya Jana Sangh, Delhi, V, 30 December 1956.
42. *Ibid.*
43. "Reorientation of Foreign Policy", Bharatiya Jana Sangh, XV All India Session, Bombay, 26 April 1969.
44. *Ibid.*
45. *Organiser, Ibid.*
46. *Times of India, Ibid.*
47. *Statesman*, Delhi, 7 June 1967.
48. *Statesman*, Delhi, 7 June 1967.
49. *Ibid.*
50. *Ibid.*
51. Editorial, *Organiser*, 11 June 1967, p 1.
52. Resolution No 67, 09, Arab-Israel War, 30 June 1967, CWC Simla, *op cit*, pp 137-138.
53. *Organiser*, Vol XXIII, No 5, September, 1969.
54. *Organiser*, Vol XXIII, No 5, September, 1969.
55. *Ibid.*
56. *Ibid.*
57. *Ibid*, Vol XXIII, No 8, 4 October 1969, p 1.
58. *Ibid.*
59. *Ibid.*
60. *Ibid.*
61. *Organiser*, Editorial "Over Rabat", Vol XXIII, October 1969.

62. Even President Giri by writing a letter to Prime Minister Indira Gandhi had condemned the government's participation in the Islamic Summit at Rabat last month, that is in the last week of October. President in his letter showed his annoyance over the stupid decision to go to Rabat and bring upon his country the humiliation, he regarded as a black mark against the Presidency. It was unconstitutional and government had not sent an official delegation to a patently religious conference. He dubbed Indira's decision as "Constitutional impropriety and against the letter and spirit of the Constitution. Even Congress MP like Mohan Dharia and Chandra Shekhar have condemned the action of the government.
63. *Organiser*, Vol XXIII, No 14, 15 November 1969, p 1.
64. Bharatiya Jana Sangh Presidential address by Atal Bihari Vajpayee at 16th All India Session Chanakya Nagar, Patna, 28 December 1969.
65. *Organiser*, Vol XXV, No 11, 23 October 1971, p 6.
66. Lok Sabha Debates, Vol XXXIII, No 1, 17 November 1969, pp 320-420.

CHAPTER 6

Bangladesh Problem: Historical Background

The Muslim League in its famous resolution of 23 March 1940 demanded the creation of Pakistan. The resolution, however, demanded not one Pakistan but two Pakistans. The resolution stated that no constitutional plan would be workable in this country or acceptable to the Muslims unless it is designed on the following basis principles, viz, that geographically contiguous units are demarcated into regions in which Muslim are numerically in a majority, as in the North-Western and Eastern Zones of India, and they should be grouped to constitute independent state in which the constituent units shall be autonomous and sovereign.[1]

This resolution thus clearly spoke to two independent and sovereign Muslim States in the Indian sub-continent. This resolution formed the political basis of the creation of Pakistan; this resolution also facilitated the emergence of Bangladesh.

Pakistan was formed on 14 August 1947 consisting of two wings which were separated by the thousand and two hundred miles of Indian territory. It was geographical incongruity. The two wings were not only far off geographically from each other but they also lacked any of those elements which constitute a nation. Islam was the only common factor between the two wings, but here also there was difference. The West Pakistan considered themselves as descendants of Muslim conquerors of India, whereas Muslims of East Pakistan were considered as converts from the low caste Hindus, and therefore, inferior Muslims.

There was glaring cultural difference between the two wings. The East Pakistan were Bengalis—they spoke Bangla language which is akin to Sanskrit whereas people of West Pakistan spoke several languages; they were culturally diversified and the Punjab and Pathans among were of pugnacious nature, whereas the Bengali gave evidence of having a fine culture and were more politically conscious. It may be mentioned that Muslim League had secured majority in British India only in Bengal. In the Muslim majority areas of western region of the British India, the Congress had won a majority of seats.

After the creation of Pakistan, there was a ruthless exploitation of East Pakistan by the West-Pakistanis. Not only Bengali Language and culture were put at a discount but most of the administrative and military posts in East Pakistan were occupied by West Pakistanis.

Naturally, there was resentment in East Pakistan. In 1954 Election the people of East Bengal dealt a death blow to the Muslim League. The United Front consisting of the Awami League of HS Suhrawardy and the Krishak Sramik Party of AK Fazlul Huq came to power and formed the government. This political development was not liked by the ruling class in West Pakistan. They soon dismissed the popular ministry and imposed Governor's rule in East Bengal.

A General Election was scheduled in 1959. This was based on the principle of one man one vote. The people of East Bengal were in overall majority in Pakistan, therefore, faithful implementation of the principle of one man one vote would have resulted in majority of East Bengalis in the National

Assembly of Pakistan. This was not acceptable to the ruling circles in West Pakistan. To prevent the election a martial law regime came in 1958. The constitution was abrogated and political parties were banned.[2]

General Ayub Khan became the President and the Martial Law Administrator of Pakistan. He named East Bengal as East Pakistan, framed a new constitution and held election on the basis of his basic democracy scheme, which had built in safeguards to favour the *status quo*.

The people of East Pakistan were suppressed. Muzibur Rahman, the leader of the Awami League, demanded maximum regional autonomy for East Pakistan on the basis of his six point programme. For this, Muzibur Rahman was arrested.

There was a wave of protest and agitation in East Pakistan. Ayub could not face this popular anger and he was replaced by General Muhammad Yahya Khan. General Yahya Khan reimposed Marshal Law and dismissed national and provincial assemblies. However, he held General Elections in December 1970.

When General Yahya Khan took the reign of government from Field Marshal Muhammad Ayub Khan, he announced that his purpose was to bring democracy in Pakistan. He announced solemnly that he had no ambition other than the creation of conditions conducive to the establishment of a constitutional government.[3]

This was a pious declaration of self-abnegation. However, it was clear from the very start that General Yahya Khan did not mean what he said. However, there was also the danger of giving public offence, if elections were to be postponed. The lessons of downfall of Ayub Khan were well taken. There was danger of people's upsurge, if dictatorship was perpetuated and elections denied. Therefore, General Elections were to be swallowed, however, unpalatable they might be; also the elections could not be made farcical as had been done by President Ayub Khan earlier in the name of basic democracy. As Mr Anthony Mascarenhas observed,

> "in this matter it was vital that justice must be done to the people."[4]

Therefore, Yahya Khan ordered for elections so that they could serve as a buffer against public protest and give regime to much needed legitimacy. However, he predetermined the pattern of new constitution which would leave his own position untouched. He banked upon endless political discord between the political parties and the politicians. There were 36 political parties and groups which were seemingly incapable of reaching any agreement at an alternative system of government. General Yahya Khan found these circumstances a convenient opportunity to further his own objective of perpetuating his hold on power.

However, while marking this assessment President Yahya Khan made a grievous mistake in forgetting the simmering discontent in the East Pakistan. As an observer has aptly remarked when General Yahya Khan

> "embarked on his adventure he did not foresee that East Bengal's economic and political grievances, arising from two decades of colonial exploitations, would assume the proportion of a tidal wave during the elections. That would even make unholy aims of the fundamental presumption of disunity on which his coup was based this was a vital mistake."[5]

And when the chips were down the assumption of political disunity proved false. So far as East Pakistan was concerned the political landscape was characterized by overwhelming political unity spearheaded by Awami League. The six-point manifesto of Awami League assumed the status of Magna Carta and the elections became an opportunity to hold a referendum on Bengali nationalism.

In the elections that were held, the people in East Pakistan voted overwhelming in favour of the Awami League, which got absolute majority in the National Assembly winning 167 out of 313 seats and captured all seats except two in East Pakistan Assembly.[6] This development threw overboard all the calculations of General Yahya Khan, he lost his political balance which he never regained.

The unprecedented victory of the Awami League of Sheikh Muzibur Rahman, and on this basis his demand for autonomy for East Bengal, was the logical sequel to the upsurge to territorial and cultural nationalism against the Islamic nationalism which had been used as an instrument for maintaining their colonial hold over East Bengal by the rulers of West Pakistan.

As the *Organiser* described, it was clear from the very moment of the victory of Awami League that East Bengal would not remain part of Pakistan for long and that the two-nation theory on the basis of which India was partitioned, would find its burial ground there.[7] As such the sympathy of all those Indians who are opposed to the two-nation theory and its pernicious implications, was naturally with Muzibur Rahman from the beginning.

The National Assembly was scheduled to meet in March 1971 but before that brutal killing, by the military, was unleashed on the unarmed people of East Pakistan. The leaders of the Awami League were arrested and women and children were subjected to unspeakable brutalities.

The people of East Pakistan declared their independence from Pakistan and proclaimed the birth of Bangladesh on 26 March 1971.

The Pakistani army had planned a final solution of East Pakistani problem. It has planned to evict the entire Hindu population of East Pakistan, which formed 10% of the total population and to liquidate the entire Muslim Bengali youth. The *Sunday Times* (London) had reported that this was a genocide conducted with amazing casualness.[8]

The Pakistan military operation resulted in over ten million refugees taking shelter in India and several thousand people were killed in East Pakistan. As *The Times* magazine reported "Pakistan's military crackdown took a terrible toll, involving perhaps 10,00,000 dead; 10 million refugees, untold thousands homeless and hungry."[9]

Pakistan declared war also on India on 1 December 1971. The liberation army of Bangladesh called the Mukti Bahini was giving a good fight to the Pakistan army and a large part of the territory of the erstwhile East Pakistan had come under the effective control of Mukti Bahini. India recognized Bangladesh on 6 December 1971. The Pakistan army led by General Niyazi signed the Instrument of Surrender of Pakistan Army to the joint military command of India and Bangladesh.

India and Bangladesh signed a 25 year pact of friendship and co-operation on 19 March 1972. Pakistan also was persuaded to recognize Bangladesh on 3 February 1974.

Attitude of Jana Sangh

The attitude of Bharatiya Jana Sangh towards this problem can be discussed in two headings—(1) attitude towards the plight of Hindus in East Pakistan, and (2) attitude towards the liberation movement of Bangladesh.

1. *Towards the Plight of Hindus in East Pakistan*

The Jana Sangh showed its concern for the future of Hindus in East Pakistan from the very beginning. It passed several resolutions and demanded territory from East Pakistan for settling the Hindu refugees that continued pouring into India from time to time.

Jana Sangh observed that the widespread atrocities against Hindus that occurred in East Pakistan made clear that under the Islamic rule of Pakistan, there was no place for those who subscribe to any non-Islamic faith. These riots were not just sporadic events but were the result of a deep-laid conspiracy to which highest officials in Pakistan had been a party.

The objective of those disturbances had been two fold. Firstly, to divert the discontent of the people of East Bengal against its domination by West Pakistan, and, secondly to pressurize and bully India in respect of Kashmir. It was evident that Hindus in Pakistan become veritable hostages in the hands of the government there. The Government of India and the Indian people were pledged to ensuring the security and honour of Hindus in Pakistan and so could not be indifferent to the situation. Pakistan was accepted on the specific condition that the Hindus in Pakistan would be treated without discrimination and that they would be guaranteed a peaceful and honourable existence.[10]

The Nehru-Liaquat Pact reaffirmed this condition. But Pakistan not only reduced Hindus to the level of second class citizens but had been systematically trying to liquidate them, with the result that during the last 14 years, over 60 lakh Hindus had to flee Pakistan and come over to India. This shows that Pakistan was not prepared to honour its commitment.[11]

Bharatiya Jana Sangh passed a resolution and said that people of India were gravely concerned over the continuously deteriorating condition of the Hindus in East Bengal. This anxiety grew all the more since it became clear that the policy of Pakistan was to drive out all those who were of strong will and to force through atrocities the weaker to embrace Islam. They were already on the move in this direction. The party wanted that India could not watch all this in silence, for it had accepted the responsibility for the protection of Hindus in Pakistan. The Hindus in Pakistan had not asked for partition but it was thrusted upon them against their wishes, and at the time of Partition leaders of India including Mahatma Gandhi, Sardar Patel and Pandit Nehru had given them the clear promise that it would be the duty of the people and the Government of India to always consider protection of their interests.[12]

At the same time, if the exodus of Hindus from East Bengal continued and if they were to take shelter in India, nearly one crore people would have to be settled and given employment, which was beyond the means of India and it would break the economic backbone of this country. That the minorities would be given civil rights and protection, was the fundamental basis of partition of India. Pakistan had deliberately thrown this fundamental-understanding to the winds. Hence, the protection of minorities in Pakistan became not only the right of India but also its duty.

Hence, Jana Sangh urged the Government of India to put forceful pressure on Pakistan for putting an end to the exodus, stop sending any type of goods to it and break commercial ties. All other steps necessary for a lasting solution of this problem should also be taken.[13]

From the very beginning, ever since the ill-advised and unfortunate partition of India at the instance of the Congress leaders 8 years ago in August 1947, there had been a continuous exodus of minorities from Pakistan into the Indian Union. So far as the West Pakistan provinces were concerned, pracucally the entire Hindu population there had to flee for their lives and come away due to the inhuman atrocities perpetuated on them. As such, there resulted an almost entire 'Exchange of Population'. No further, exodus from West Pakistan was now taking place.

But the situation with regard to East Bengal was different. In this area, there had been no such exchange of population. It had been really a out way traffic-Hindus from East Bengal were coming away, but no Muslim of the (Purbanchal) Eastern Zone (West Bengal, Assam, Bihar and Orissa) were leaving for East Bengal. In fact, in West Bengal itself around 50 lakh Muslims are residing.[14]

This time, the exodus had affected not merely the educated ones but also the agricultural and artisan classes which were usually rooted to the soil and scarcely took any interest in politics. The big exodus of the Hindu masses still continued in alarming dimensions.

The reasons were obvious. The Hindus in East Bengal, both masses and classes alike were convinced that so long as Pakistan existed and was ruled as on Islamic state, there was no room for Hindus there to live a decent and honourable life. They were oppressed and suppressed in thousand ways. Their complaints went unheeded by the authorities, their economic life was strangled and their cultural and educational life was sought to be perverted.

In spite of the Congress government's tendency not to face the unpleasant facts and indeed to suppress them, this most unhappy state of affairs was brought home to the Deputy Minister of External Affairs of the Government of India, when he was on a tour through East Bengal some months ago. He had to admit it.[15]

Jana Sangh felt that abiding solution to this baffling problem of refugees from Pakistan could be satisfactorily solved only when the unnatural partition was annulled and the refugees were honourably reinstalled in their home lands. But pending that solution, the government had an inescapable duty towards these refugees, because it was the Government of India which was responsible for their present condition. It has to see that the refugees from East Bengal were properly helped and rehabilitated. The Jana Sangh demanded that:

(i) Adequate steps should be taken to rehabilitate the Hindu refugees from East Bengal, so that they can become economically self-supporting and stand on their own legs and become useful members of society instead of remaining as helpless and floating derelicts without any hope for future.

(ii) In the matter of resettlement of refugees from East Bengal, care should be taken that piece meal settlement of isolated families in uncongenial and unsuitable surrounding are avoided.

(iii) Immediate steps be taken by the Government of India to realize from Pakistan Government the full value of the assets and properties left by the Hindus in East Bengal and to create out of this a 'compensation fund' from which the refugees are to be paid the full value of the properties left behind by them.

(iv) The refugees from Pakistan must be given full citizenship in India automatically without the troublesome procedure of registration, etc.

(v) The Policy of auctioning the shops and tenements so far built to rehabilitate refugees to the highest bidder must be given up, as, it would displace many of refugees once again. Such shops and tenements should be transferred to their present refugee occupants on a no profit and no loss basis.

(vi) A high-power commission should be set up to go into the entire question of the rehabilitation of refugees from both wings of Pakistan to ascertain the extent to

> which the problem has been solved and to suggest ways and means for the speedy and effective completion of the remaining rehabilitation work.[16]

The Party said that under these circumstances the only course left to India was that it prepares to rehabilitate the Hindus who were still in Pakistan and for this purpose it should demand from Pakistan necessary territory and full compensation of their properties left behind.

2. *Towards the Liberation Movement of Bangladesh*

The Bharatiya Jana Sangh observed that the development in East Bengal since 1 December 1971, when Awami League of Muzibur Rahman was returned to power with a massive majority in Pakistan National Assembly and East Bengal Assembly, though unprecedented in their magnitude are the logical sequel to the creation of the monstrous absurdity called Pakistan on the basis of two-nation theory by the Muslim League and the Congress twenty-four years back. A philosophy or ideology which assumed that Dacca could feel itself closer to Lahore and Islamabad 1,200 miles away than to Calcutta—and that a citizen of East Bengal could find greater affinity with a citizen of West Punjab than with his next door non-Muslim Bengali neighbour is as preposterous as it is illogical, unscientific and unrealistic.

Jana Sangh remarked that any nationalist government in India would have welcomed these developments and extended all help—moral, material and diplomatic, to the people of Awami League on considerations of humanitarianism, preservation of democratic norms and values and safeguarding of our defence and national interests.

Had the Government of India acted in time, Bangladesh would have been a reality by now and much of the holocaust, genocide atrocities against children, mass rape of women and forcible squeeze out of over 70 lakh people, could have been avoided.[17]

The ruling Junta of Pakistan launched a virtual aggression against India by forcing 70 lakh refugees, with all economic, political and emotional implication of such massive and unprecedented exodus which is still continuing. At the same time Pakistan's armed forces have been intruding in border incursions, violation of Indian air space, and committing other acts of aggression with impunity. According to the Government of India's own admission, scores of Indian civilians and armed personnel have been killed by such indiscriminate incurious and intrusions into our territory by Pakistan's armed forces. Massive preparations are also being made by Pakistan to launch an aggression in Kashmir and other vulnerable parts of western India during a time and place of her choosing.

The Jana Sangh remarked that the government of Smt Gandhi, like Chamberlain's government in UK in 1939, was trying to evade its duty through appeasement of Pakistan and General Yahya Khan, who had excelled Hitler as far as barbarism and cruelty over people is concerned. The leadership of a country is tested at the time of crisis. In this crisis of her tenure in office, Smt Gandhi has proved that she cannot lead the country. The interests of the country are not safe in her hands. Instead of giving a positive lead to her cabinet, Parliament and the people she had been wasting valuable time by sending cabinet Ministers to world capitals with wagging tongues and begging bowls to canvas sympathy for India and beg help for the refugees.[18]

How miserably such missions failed, was proved by the way USA allowed ships laden with military hardware for Pakistan to sail as soon as Sardar Swaran Singh left Washington. While the attitude of the Government of USA deserves strongest condemnation, it has also clearly proved that there is no place for any principles, charity or morality in international relations. Every country was guided by its own national interests and not by any other consideration. As things were Pakistan was a member of SEATO and CENTO. The USA and UK, therefore, strive to maintain its unity as a counterbalance to India. Even USSR was maintaining an attitude of non-alignment between India and Pakistan.[19]

The Bharatiya Jana Sangh observed that the Government of India should have taken immediate steps to help Bangladesh on the following lines—

(i) Immediate recognition should have been given to the democratically elected government of Swadhin Bangladesh and effective moral and material should be given it to normalize conditions there soon and efforts be made for early release of Sheikh Muzibur Rahman and others under arrest.

(ii) Dispersal of the displaced persons to far off places should be stopped. As far as possible camps for the refugees should be put on the Bangladesh border so that they might go back to their homes as soon as Pakistani army of occupation is thrown out of Bangladesh. Screening should be done to detect Pakistani agents and other undesirable elements amongst the refugees. Young men amongst them should be given military training.

(iii) Effective military action is taken to repel Pakistani aggression on our borders.

(iv) Effective curbs should be put on Sheikh Abdullah, Majlis-e-Mushawarat, Tameer-e-Millat and Jamaat-e-Islami, Muslim League and other elements who have constantly refused to condemn the military Junta for its genocide in Bangladesh. Action should be taken against newspapers etc who have supported Pakistan instead of representing national sentiments over the issue.

(v) Steps should be taken to secure co-operation of all patriotic organizations and elements in the task of repelling Pakistan's aggression securing justice for the people of Bangladesh and safeguarding the honour, integrity and security of India.

(vi) A basic reappraisal of India's foreign policy of all its aspects must be undertaken.[20]

Thus, Bharatiya Jana Sangh directed all its units to educate and mobilize public opinion in support of these demands so that government may be forced to act in the wider interests of the country. Jana Sangh also appeals to the people to extend full moral and material support to mitigate the sufferings of the displaced persons.

The Party charged the Government of India with having betrayed the cause of Bangladesh. Foreign Minister Sardar Swaran Singh's statement at Simla calling for "a political settlement within the framework of Pakistan" is a shameful let down. This anti-climactic statement serves only to highlight the ruling Congress's utter incapacity to protect national interest and its subservience to the Super Powers in the matter of national decision making.

The Bharatiya Jana Sangh remarked that the former Prime Minister of India promised the nation that the refugees from Bangladesh would return to their motherland within 6 months. The six months' period has elapsed, but the refugees instead of being in a position to return, are streaming in larger number. With the end of the Monsoons, General Yahya's tanks will begin to mow-down the people leading to fresh atrocities and a heavier influx into this country. The near famine conditions prevailing in Bangladesh today would only aggravate the problem.

The Bharatiya Jana Sangh reacted to the Indo-Soviet Treaty of August last, the Party said that the Treaty would be judged not only by its wordings but by its working, and that so far as India is concerned the touchstone for assessing the Treaty's worth would be its efficacy in helping resolve the Bangladesh problem. Sardar Swaran Singh's statement is a pointer that the Treaty has not helped us in this matter, it is seriously restricting our freedom of action. It has compelled us to renounce support to the cause of Bangladesh, which is independence and to acquiesce in Soviet Russia's keenness to preserve the present framework of a united Pakistan, a keenness ardently shared by the USA.

Thus the former Prime Minister had been at pains to prove that the Indo-Soviet Treaty has in no way abridged India's freedom of action with regard to Bangladesh and that the Government of India's policy had not been influenced by Russia's attitudes in this regard.[21]

When the Bangladesh problem assumed a critical form, Jana Sangh demanded and advocated giving active assistance first to the 'liberation' and then recognition of the independent Government of Bangladesh.

Vajpayee further said,

> "Yahya Khan and his henchmen are guilty of genocide in East Bengal. They are enemies of humanity and representatives of bestiality. They have transgressed the principles contained in the United Nations Charter. The barbarities committed by them can be compared with the War crimes of the Nazis. It is, therefore, a matter of surprise that no country is prepared to condemn the rulers of West Pakistan in clear terms, let alone putting them in the dock. Even the Government of India is hesitating to raise the question of the Bangladesh genocide at the UNO."[22]

Vajpayee rejected the contention that what was happening in East Pakistan was the intended victory of Pakistan. He said,

> "Pakistan's claim that the problem of East Bengal is their internal problem is utterly baseless. Till 1947, East Bengal was a part of undivided India. As a result of conspiracy of the imperialists and the weakness of Congress leaders, partition was foisted on the people of India against their wishes. But the establishment of a separate State cannot put an end to our cultural, historical and traditional ties with the people of East Bengal. India has always condemned the economic exploitation and political repression of East Bengal by West Pakistan. We have lauded and wished success to the brave struggle of East Bengal for democratic liberties. Today when Pakistani rulers are bent upon drowning East Bengal in a sea of blood and tears, India would be proving false to its ideals of democracy and freedom if it remains content with paying lip service to the cause of East Bengal."[23]

Vajpayee deplored the delay in the positive response of Indian government to these events and said,

> "It is a bitter fact that in the case of East Bengal, the Government of India has already indulged in inordinate delay. When the Pakistan army started a massacre in Dacca on March 25 it should have been clear to the government that lakhs of people would take refuge in India to escape death. The oppression and resultant exodus of Hindus from East Bengal that we had been witnessing during the last 24 years should have been a sufficient pointer to future events. Further, the targets of Pakistani wrath this time were not only the Hindus but also the leaders and supporters of the Awami League who had decided not to suffer the life of injustice and want, and not to let East Bengal continue as a colony of Islamabad."

Proving a lesson from the history, Vajpayee said,

> "The massacres before and after the establishment of Pakistan, during which lakhs of people were killed and crores became homeless, the constant effort, after eliminating all non-Muslims from West Pakistan, to systematically squeeze out Hindus from East Bengal, as result of which 1,80,00,000 Hindus of East Bengal were either driven to India, or killed or forcibly converted; the infiltration of Pakistani Muslims in the border areas of Assam, West Bengal and Bihar, which is meant to make them Muslim majority areas and finally parts of Pakistan; Pakistani aid to anti-national elements in the Naga and Mizo areas in the form of arms and military training; all these facts should have easily convinced New Delhi that the rulers of Pakistan would deal with the revolution in East Bengal in a manner such as to attempt killing two birds with one stone. On the one hand they would try to liquidate all those who demanded freedom and equality, and on the other, by driving millions of refugees into India, they would precipitate a situation that would gravely endanger the economy, political stability and law and order in our country."[24]

After touring the border areas of East Bengal in the second week of April, I had suggested to government leaders that enough assistance should be immediately given to the Liberation Army to enable it to declare a territory adjacent to the Indian border as a 'Liberated Zone' and make arrangement for its defence. It was asked then; where is the Government of Bangladesh which could be given military assistance? But when an independent sovereign Bangladesh government was established on 15 April, New Delhi began to say how can we give aid to Bangladesh government so long as we do not recognize it? And when a demand to recognize it was made, we were told that the time has not come to do so. It is also said that recognizing Bangladesh would be harmful for its own interest, as if Bangladesh leaders, who are demanding recognition, do not know where their interest lie.

Vajpayee demanded an end to the policy of drift and indecision followed by India. He said,

> "It is clear that government's policy regarding Bangladesh has been one of drift since the very beginning. New Delhi neither knows what its aim is, nor what it should do to achieve that aim. Had the influx of refugees not being lip sympathy to the cause of East Bengal was all that was required for it to discharge its duty."

He further observed,

> "The Government of India must clearly say whether it wants East Bengal to be free or whether it wants a solution in which East Bengal remains a part of Pakistan. So far as the people of East Bengal are concerned, they are not prepared to strike a compromise on anything less than freedom. Nazrul Islam, Acting President of Independent Bangladesh, has clearly stated; "Pakistan is dead, and now it cannot be revived." Is the Government of India pledge to keep Pakistan in one piece, as are Britain, America and Communist China? If not, it must declare in clear terms that it wants East Bengal to take its place in the comity of nations as a free and sovereign country and for this purpose it would give every assistance to the freedom fighters."

Vajpayee cautioned against the trap of 'political solution'. He said,

> "The constant repetition of the phrase 'political solution' by New Delhi lends strength to the suspicion that the

> Government of India does not want East Bengal to be free, and that there is no difference between its point of view and the point of view of those big powers which are bent upon saving Pakistan from disintegration. One can understand the pro-Pakistan policy of Britain, America, China and Russia. They do not want Pakistan to fall apart or to become weak, because they want to use Pakistan for the purpose of keeping India under check. But the question is why should India be so solicitous about the survival of a state which was born out of hatred and contempt for India, which has always considered India its enemy number one, which has openly aggressed upon India three times, which always keeps dreaming of usurping Jammu-Kashmir, an integral part of India, and thus effecting a second partition, which has exploited every single opportunity to incite communal riots in our country, and which has no scrapes and is willing to go any length to damn India in the eyes of the world?"

He further adumbrated,

> "The people of India can never forget that the partition of 1947 marked a tremendous failure of our national movement. In their hurry to attain independence for the country, the leadership of those days acquiesced in the sin of partition; today, an opportunity has presented itself to make amends for the deed. The wheel has turned full circle. On that occasion, India has been divided into two on the basis of religion. Today, religion cannot prevent Pakistan from breaking up into two. The partition of Pakistan is a natural as the partition of India was unnatural. Religion cannot after facts of geography, nor can it serve cultural and historical links. In Europe, Christian States have been fighting with one another for centuries. In West Asia many Muslim countries are even today at

> daggers drawn. The basis on which Pakistan was created is completely hollow. Pakistan is being buried under its own burden misdeeds. The Government of India should not do anything that would hinder this historical process of the disintegration of Pakistan. In fact, it is government's duty to promote this process.[25]

He said,

> "The Government of India must make clear what it means by a 'political solution'. It must also indicate a deadline for this so-called political solution. Time is on the side of Pakistan, and Pakistan is attempting not a political solution but a final solution. Those East Bengalis who may survive the massacre and exodus would be silenced by terror or temptation. After that it would not be difficult for Pakistan to set up a puppet government of Muslim League and Jamaat-e-Islami supporters. Since a few days the rulers of Pakistan have already started claiming that the situation in East Bengal is returning to normal. They are also making much ado about evacuees returning to Reception centres. Countries which are anxious to find a solution of the East Bengal problem within the framework of Pakistan would be only too glad to lean upon these false and mischievous claims."

The Prime Minister and her companions must realize this clearly that the 'political solution of the East Bengal problem which the people there would like will never be acceptable to Pakistan. The six-point programme on which the Awami League fought the election and secured a majority not only in East Bengal but in the whole of Pakistan can no longer be a basis of agreement. It would be acceptable neither to Islamabad nor to the Awami League, or would it open the door for the return of evacuees. There is no alternative before India except to give every possible assistance for the success of East

Bengali's freedom struggle, if this leads to war with Pakistan, India should be ready for it.

Pakistan has already declared war on India by pushing lakhs of its citizens into India. But India cannot permit Pakistan to endanger our economy and political stability for a solution of its own problem. India must give an effective reply to this aggression by Pakistan. If the big powers of the world are with us, with them, if they prefer to remain silent spectators, without them; and if they oppose, in spite of their opposition, India will have to do its duty. We cannot let East Bengali die. We cannot betray the land of Gurudev Rabindra Nath and Kazi Nazarul Islam. We shall not allow the flame of freedom democracy and communal harmony which the brave people of East Bengal have lighted their great leader Sheikh Muzibur Rahman to be smothered.

It warned the Government of India that the patience of the people is running out. The country does not want high-sounding slogans; it wants concrete and effective action. The people of India are prepared for any hardship and sacrifice for the freedom of East Bengal. The government must give up its vacillating policy and firmly determine itself on a bold step.

The Jana Sangh felt that it had special link with the problems of East Bengal and hence special responsibility. Vajpayee said

> "The Bharatiya Jana Sangh has a special link with the problem of East Bengal. Dr Syama Prasad Mukherjee, founder of the Jana Sangh, had resigned from independent India's first cabinet in 1950 in protest against the government's weak policy on the exodus of Hindus from East Bengal. Had the government needed his warming and changed its policy towards Pakistan we would not have faced with the present serious situation. There is still time. Let the government awake and transform Pakistan's

> challenge into a great opportunity. Such opportunities to change the course of history do not only would Bangladesh be destroyed but the security, peace and progress of India also would be imperilled."

Vajpayee advocated reorientation of India's foreign policy to suit the needs of our policy regarding Bangladesh. He said,

> "The dismal response for the cause of Bangladesh has once again highlighted the need to reorient India's foreign policy. This is not the first occasion when India has found itself totally friendless in the world. Even those countries that we backed in their hour of distress have rejected our approaches. The attitude adopted by Arab countries to the Bangladesh question is an instance in point. Let us, therefore, realize that hard realism, and not starry romanticism, can be the basis of a successful foreign policy."[26]
>
> The Prime Minister and other government spokesmen had been telling the people that recognition of an independent sovereign Bangladesh was quite on the cards but that the timing of such a decision should be left to the government.[27]

Jana Sangh observed that, the Bangladesh problem was much more than a humanitarian problem, as the international community would like us to believe. The problem vitally affects our security, our economy and our political stability. But even if the return of the refugees were to be regarded as our main interest in the question, it must be understood quite clearly that no refugee is going to return unless Bangladesh is liberated from Yahya Khan's shackles and Pakistan's troops are withdrawn from Bangladesh.[28]

Jana Sangh observed that if any one talks about a settlement "Within the framework of Pakistan" that very movement he is ruling out both these postulates, and thus negating all possibility the return of refugees.[29]

The party remarked that the 1966 Tashkent Pact, was betrayal of the sacrifices made by our valiant jawans.

The Tashkent Pact of the offing would be a betrayal not only on the brave freedom fighters of Bangladesh and many others who have laid down their lives for the cause but also of India's own national interests.[30]

Thus, the Bharatiya Jana Sangh called upon all nationalist and democratic forces, which have been urging immediate recognition of Bangladesh to make a concrete effort to prevent this capitulation.

The Bangladesh issue was a great challenge to Jana Sangh in many respects. Jana Sangh was accused from the very beginning as being an inveterate enemy of everything of Pakistan, and at the same time being anti-Muslim also.

Any impression of continuing the anti-Muslim policy would have played into the hands of Pakistan, because the Pakistan tried from the very beginning to sow the seeds of communal bitterness in the erstwhile East Pakistan, and to turn the Bangladesh problem into an Indo-Pakistan problem.

In the pursuance of this policy Pakistan drove away millions of Hindu refugees to India. It also tried to instigate communal passions and communal riots in India. The situation called for a very sophisticated response from Jana Sangh. Jana Sangh recognized the complexity of this situation and responded accordingly.

Jana Sangh pleaded for early recognition of Bangladesh and giving it armed assistance. It refused to regard the problem of Pakistan crackdown on Bangladesh as Hindu-Muslim problem. Atal Bihari Vajpayee said that the Pakistan army was not only annihilating the Hindus of Bangladesh but also the

Muslims. That it was not a question of suffering of Hindus at the hands of the Muslim rather it was a question of Pakistani colonial suppression of resurgent Bangladesh.

There was exodus of refugees from the erstwhile East Pakistan into India. The Working Committee of the Jana Sangh met at Chandigarh on 16-17 July 1970, and urged the Government of India to ask Pakistan to provide land for the rehabilitation of the refugees pouring from East Pakistan to India.[31]

Later on Atal Bihari Vajpayee, President of Jana Sangh, asked the members of the Jana Sangh to work for communal peace and said that the Pakistani rulers were torturing and exterminating not only the Hindu population of East Pakistan but also the Muslim population. He said "let us not fall into the trap of Pakistan. We must see that there is no communal incident." He further said that "there was no doubt that brutalities and atrocities were being perpetrated on the East Pakistan, and particularly, against the Hindu population there."

But he warned that

> "we should not be provoked by this, we have no quarrel with Muslims living in India. If we have to retaliate, it will be against the Pakistan government. Our fight is not with the Muslims but with the military regime directing these brutalities and genocide from Pakistan."[32]

The Bangladesh problem caused a great metamorphosis in the traditional attitude of the Jana Sangh. There were Assembly Elections in 1972 and the Muslims in Bihar felt very much concerned about the fate of those Muslim in Bangladesh who had migrated from Bihar and settled in East Pakistan. The new Government of Bangladesh regarded these Bihari Muslims as collaborators of Pakistan and was against their remaining in Bangladesh. On the other hand the Pakistani government also was unwilling to accept them.

Thakur Prasad a prominent Jana Sangh leader of Bihar had declared in a rally of Muslims at Patna that the Bihari Muslims should be allowed to return to Bihar. This was a Jana Sangh bid to stop alienation of Muslim voters from Jana Sangh and to woo them. Indira Gandhi, the then Prime Minister of India, bitterly criticized this stand of Jana Sangh and declared that India would never accept these 'Bihari Muslims', because they have acted as the worst criminals in collaboration with the West Pakistan army in the erstwhile East Pakistan.

Thus, the Jana Sangh bid to woo the Muslim voters in Bihar was refuted by the Congress bid to cause of backlash of Hindu voters against Jana Sangh.

Pakistan had launched a diabolical campaign to eliminate the Hindu population of East Pakistan by either driving out the Hindu population as refugees from East Pakistan or killing them. The result was that millions of Hindus of East Pakistan were forced to take shelter as refugees in India. There was a great crisis. India with its strained resources was forced to feed these helpless refugees and take care of them. The situation was intolerable. Even the continuation of such a situation would have sounded a death knell of the Indian economy.

Prof Madhok advocated that the battle for Bangladesh is battle against two-nation theory and communalism. That is the importance and significance of the development in Bangladesh for India.[33]

Dr Bhai Mahavir said that Bangladesh was not an internal matter of Pakistan, just as Goa was not an internal matter of Portugal. In case of Bangladesh, it has larger population than West Pakistan. Thus the majority cannot be accused of secession or treason. The Jana Sangh was convinced that the proud Bengalis were not going to give in to the gulf dividing them from the West Pakistan. This gulf had been immeasurably deepened and widened, and in 1971 it was full to the form with the blood and tears of the freedom fighters. Therefore, Jana Sangh said that delay in recognition of Bangladesh by India would only prolong its agony. Further the delay would also be fatal for the democratic elements of Bangladesh. If the fight was prolonged, the democratic elements would be eliminated and communists would take over. That would bring China at India's eastern door step. Jana Sangh organized a Satyagrah for recognition of Bangladesh from 1 August to 12 August 1971 in Delhi, and it also organized a mammoth rally in Delhi.

Atal Bihari Vajpayee addressed a rally and said that war with Pakistan was inevitable. It was a question of only selecting time by India or leaving to Pakistan. In warfare choosing one's time may sometime make all the difference between victory and defeat.[34]

Lal Chand Sabharwal, Vice-President Punjab Jana Sangh said that the Satyagraha offered by the Jana Sangh was aimed not to embarrass the Central Government but to strengthen the hands of Prime Minister Indira Gandhi and induce to do justice to the 75 million people of Bangladesh, who were fighting against brutal injustice.[35]

Nearly 600 Muslims also demonstrated before the house of the Prime Minister in support of the Jana Sangh demand for immediate recognition of Bangladesh. The demonstration was led by Anwar Ali Dehlvi, Secretary of the Jana Sangh party in the Metropolitan Council. The Muslim demonstrators presented a memorandum which said that the demand for the recognition of Bangladesh is the secular demand and anybody who opposes it strikes at secularism and houses the fires of communalism.[36]

Addressing the Jana Sangh rally in Delhi on 8 August 1971, Atal Bihari Vajpayee said

> "Recognition of Bangladesh has already been delayed inordinately. More delay would mean being taken in with open eyes by the Pakistani conspiracy to present the Bangladesh problem as a problem between India and Pakistan. So long as we do not recognize the independent existence of Bangladesh, Pakistan will keep trying to drag India into the international forum on the plea that all the assistance given to the Mukti Bahini amounts to Indian interference in the internal affairs of Pakistan. Official recognition by India would on the one hand help Bangladesh achieve international status, and enable it to get Indian assistance—diplomatic economic as well as military.[37]

The Jana Sangh passed an elaborate resolution on the Bangladesh situation. Analysing the course of events there, the Jana Sangh resolution noted the collapse of the unnatural two-nation theory. It said, "The developments in East Bengal since 1 December, when Awami League of Muzibur Rahman returned to power with a massive majority in Pakistan National Assembly and East Bengal Assembly, though unprecedented in their magnitude and barbarism are the logical sequel to the creation of monstrous absurdity called Pakistan on the basis of two-nation theory of the Muslim League and the Congress 24 years back. A philosophy or ideology which assumed that Dacca could feel itself closer to Lahore and Islamabad 1,200 miles away than to Calcutta and that a citizen of East Bengal could find greater affinity with a citizen of West Punjab than with his next door non-Muslim Bengali neighbour is as preposterous as it is illogical, unscientific and unrealistic.

This ideology began to collapse soon after the partition. The revival of the movement for Pakhtunistan, the anti-Urdu riots in Dacca, the massive victory of Fazlul Haq in the first general elections held in Pakistan in 1954 and revival of Sindhi consciousness as distinct from Muslim or Pakistani consciousness were early symptoms of the present development in East Bengal and their ramification is Sindh, Baluchistan and Pakhtunistan.

These developments have exploded the two-nation theory as nothing else could have done and destroyed the very basis on which Pakistan was created by partitioning India. They are harbingers of the end of Pakistan and re-unification of what God and nature has made one.[38]

Deploring in action on the part of Government of India, the resolution said,

> "Any nationalist government in India would have welcomed these developments and extended all help, moral material and diplomatic, to the people of Awami League on considerations of humanitarianism, defence and preservation of democratic norms and values and safeguarding of our national interest. Had the Government of India acted in time, Bangladesh would have been a reality by now and much of the holocaust, genocide, atrocities against children, mass rape of women and forcible squeeze-out of over seven million people, mostly Hindus could have been avoided."

Jana Sangh noted the three nefarious objectives of Pakistan in the Bangladesh crisis. It said "The inaction and indecision on the part of the Government of India encouraged the military Junta of Pakistan to start its unprecedented measure in Pakistan with three set objectives." The first objective as Mr Anthony Mascarenhas spelled out so clearly is to exterminate all those who had dared to challenge in any shape or from the basic ideology of Pakistan. That explain their special effort to kill the intellectuals, students and professors and youth in general who had heralded the movement of Bangladesh.

Second aim was to cut down the population of East Bengal to enforce the principle of parity between West Pakistan and East Bengal in any future constitution of Pakistan.

The third objective was to eliminate every Hindu from East Bengal as they had done in West Punjab to make East Bengal into a homogeneous Islamic area with no trace of heresy. To that end nearly one crore Hindus of East Bengal have been systematically exterminated or squeezed out highest level at Islamabad is clear from the writings of *Pakistan Times*, the official organ of the Government of Pakistan and report of Michael Hornby from Dacca, published in *The Times*, London on 23 June 1971 under the capital 'Systematic Hunt for Hindus'.

Another objective of Pakistan's policy seems to be to strike terror in the hearts of nationalism of Sindh, Baluchistan and Pakhtunistan so that they may not dare to emulate the example of the nationalists of Bangladesh.

The Jana Sangh resolution further said,

> "As things are the ruling Junta of Pakistan has launched a virtual aggression against India by forcing seven million refugees, mostly Hindus, with all economic, political and emotional implications of such massive and unprecedented exodus which is still continuing. At the same time Pakistan's armed forces have been indulging in border incursions, violation of Indian air space and committing other acts of aggression with impunity. According to the Government of India's own admission, scores of India civilians and armed personnel have been killed by such indiscriminate incursions and intrusions into our territory by Pakistan's armed forces. Massive preparation were also being made by Pakistan to launch an aggression in Kashmir and other vulnerable parts of Western India at a time and place of her choosing.

Instead of taking steps to meet this aggression, Indira Gandhi's government, like Chamberlain Government in UK in 1939, is trying to evade its duty through appeasement of Pakistan and Yahya Khan, who had excelled Hitler as far as barbarism and cruelty over people is concerned.

> "Instead of giving a positive lead to her Cabinet, Parliament and the people she has been wasting valuable time by sending cabinet ministers to world capitals with wagging tongues and begging bowls to canvas sympathy for India and the refugees, How miserably such missions have failed is proved by the way USA allowed ships laden with military hardware for Pakistan to sail as soon as Swaran Singh left Washington. While the attitude of USA deserves strongest condemnation, it has also clearly proved that there is no place for any principles, charity or morality in international relations. Every country is guided by its own national interests and not by any other consideration. Pakistan is a member of SEATO and CENTO. The USA and UK therefore, would like to maintain its unity as counter-balance of India."

Discussing the lack of international support to the cause of Bangladesh, Jana Sangh resolution said,

> "Even USSR is maintaining an attitude of non-alignment between India and Pakistan."

The attitude of Arab and other Muslim countries should also be no surprise. It is just in line with the attitude they adopted at the time of Chinese aggression in 1962 and Pakistan aggression on India in 1965.

The net result of all these developments is that Pakistan feels encouraged to go ahead with its plans. The broadcast of Yahya Khan in which he has spelled out this plan about a new constitution made by experts, disqualification of Awami

League members and establishment of a puppet regime at Dacca is to whitewash the whole carnage and present the world with the fait accompli. Her friends are also watching the development and will bail her out at the first opportunity. This has made all talk of political settlement with Bangladesh meaningless. Political settlement can and must be made only with Muzibur Rahman and his Awami League and not with the puppets of Yahya Khan.

In these circumstances, it was the considered view of the Bharatiya Jana Sangh that the Government of India must take immediate steps on the following lines:

(i) Immediate recognition must be given to the democratically elected government of Swadhin Bangladesh and effective moral and material help should be given to it to normalize conditions in East Bengal and efforts be made for the release of Sheikh Muzibur Rahman and others under arrest.

(ii) Dispersal of the displaced persons to far off places should be stopped. As far as possible camps for the refugees should be put up on the Bangladesh border so that they might go back to their homes as soon as Pakistani army of occupation is thrown out of Bangladesh. Screening should be done to detect Pakistani agents amongst them should be given military training.

(iii) Effective military action must be taken to repel Pakistan aggression on our borders.

(iv) Effective curb be put on Sheikh Abdullah, Majlis-e-Mushawarat, Tameer-e-Millat and Jamaat-e-Islami, Muslim League and other elements who have consistently refused to condemn the military Junta for its genocide in Bangladesh. Action should be taken against papers which have supported Pakistan instead of representing national sentiments over the issue.

(v) Steps should be taken to secure co-operation of all patriotic organization and elements in the task of repelling Pak aggression, securing Justice for the people of Bangladesh and safeguarding the honour, integrity and security of India.

(vi) A basic reappraisal of India's foreign policy in all its aspects must be undertaken.

In support of this policy, the Jana Sangh called for mobilizing popular opinion. Its resolution said:

> "Bharatiya Jana Sangh calls upon all its units to educate and mobilize public opinion in support of these demands so that government may be forced to act in the wider interests of the country. Jana Sangh also appeals to the people to extend full moral and material help to mitigate the suffering of the displaced persons."[40]

Atal Bihari Vajpayee said that there was no alternative before India except to give every possible assistance for the success of East Bengal's freedom struggle. If this lead to war with Pakistan, India should be ready for it.[41] Bharatiya Jana Sangh criticized Indian government that a political solution to be found within the framework of Pakistan. Central Working Committee of Bharatiya Jana Sangh said on 9 October 1971 that it was shameful, there would no Bangladesh within the framework of Pakistan. It said that the Government of India betrayed the cause of Bangladesh. The statement of Indian Foreign Minister Swaran Singh at Simla was climatic and subservient to super-power pressure when the Government of India had said that the refugees will be back within six months but they are now increasing more and more. This problem virtually affects India's security, economy and political stability. There was no solution of the problem unless and until Pakistan forces withdrew from Bangladesh. The Bharatiya Jana Sangh demanded immediate recognition of Bangladesh.[42]

Criticising the limited assistance to Mukti Bahini of Bangladesh by Indian Government, Bharatiya Jana Sangh in its All India Central Council meeting (Ghaziabad) passed resolution and said, that

> "here is a situation whose solution brought neither delay nor half-heartedness. Government of India was responsible to the situation and it did not measure up to the challenge posed. Its policy of limited assistance to the Mukti Bahini was necessarily prolonging the agony of Bangladesh and was contributing besides to swelling of the number of refugees."[43]

General Council of the Jana Sangh passed a resolution. It said the development in Bangladesh "have exploded the two-nation theory as nothing else could have done and destroyed the very basis on which Pakistan was created by positioning India. The General Council further said that any nationalist government in India would have welcomed these developments and extended all help—moral, material and diplomatic, to the people of Awami League on considerations of humanitarianism, defence and preservation of democratic norms, and values and safeguarding of our national interests. Had the Government of India acted in time, Bangladesh would have been a reality by now and much of the holocaust, genocide, atrocities against children, mass rape of women and forcible squeeze out of over seven million people, mostly Hindus, could have been avoided.[45]

The emergence of Bangladesh was whole-heartedly welcomed by the Jana Sangh. A resolution passed by the party said,

> "A philosophy or ideology which assumed that Dacca could feel itself closer to Lahore and Islamabad some 1200 miles away from them to Calcutta and that a citizen of East

> Bengal could find greater affinity with citizen of West Punjab than with his next door non-Muslim Bengali neighbour is as preposterous as it is illogical, unscientific and unrealistic."[46]

Therefore, the General Council demanded immediate recognition of Bangladesh and effective moral and material help to this country.

When Pakistan declared war on India on 4 December 1971 Jana Sangh gave a call to strengthen hands of the Government of India and when India recognized Bangladesh on 6 December 1971 Jana Sangh congratulated the government on its wise decision.

After the independence of Bangladesh, Madhok advocated that there should be open frontiers between India and Bangladesh, a common market, and a policy of common defence. There must be an Indo-Bangladesh treaty having all those points included in it.

Immediately after release of Sheikh Muzibur Rahman from imprisonment in Pakistani jail, he came to New Delhi and was accorded a public reception. At that function the Jana Sangh as well the Jana Sangh's Mayor were excluded. Dr Bhai Mahavir, a Jana Sangh leader objected to the exclusion of Jana Sangh in debate in the Rajya Sabha. Smt Indira Gandhi, the Prime Minister flared up and remarked that

> "Sheikh Muzibur Rahman, I am sure, would not have approved of any communal organization being present there."

This remark provoked a valley of protests and walkouts by the Jana Sangh group from the Rajya Sabha.

Atal Bihari Vajpayee wrote a letter to the Prime Minister on 17 April 1972 and said that

> "her remarks were totally uncalled for, against parliamentary propriety and betrayed only a deep rooted animus against my party."[47]

Vajpayee further remarked that

> "When Bangladesh freedom movement was on, I had a occasion to meet and talk to a number of prominent leaders of the movement close to Sheikh Sahib and all of them were unreservedly appreciative of the efforts the Jana Sangh was making to mobilize India's public opinion in support of the Bangladesh cause in general and recognition of Bangladesh in particular."

The Central Working Committee of BJS paid its tearful tributes to the memory of thousands of soldiers, sailors and airmen who laid down their lives for the defence of India and the liberation of Bangladesh. Their glorious performance was described as a golden page in the Indian History.

The Jana Sangh advocated that the proper rehabilitation of their families, suitable employment to the wounded and satisfactory education to their children must be the first responsibility of the State.[48]

Jana Sangh was worried by reports about maiming and murder of Indian soldiers captured by Pakistanis. These fears were confirmed by the fact that while 2,163 jawans were missing, Pakistan claimed to hold less than 600 of them. The Working Committee called upon the government to take the assistance of the Red Cross and other appropriate agencies to ascertain facts and demand punishment of the guilty.[49]

The Bharatiya Jana Sangh objected that the civilians, particularly in the border areas also suffered the loss of life, limb and property. It advocated that their rehabilitation and compensation must also be undertaken by the government.

While Bangladesh had been liberated, and more than half of the refugees have gone back, the Indian Government continued to collect refugee taxes. Jana Sangh was of the definite opinion that the high cost of the reconstruction of Bangladesh put at a minimum of Rs. 600 crore by experts should be paid by Pakistan and not by India. To this end, adequate reparation should be an integral part of any true agreement with Pakistan.[50]

Attitude Towards Simla Pact

The birth of Bangladesh found 90,000 Pakistani prisoners-of-war in Indian hands, and a good chunk of territory of West Pakistan under the Indian occupation. Pakistan had only a small strip of Indian land under its occupation in the Kashmir sector.

Pakistan's immediate worry was to secure the release of Pakistani prisoners-of-war from India and get them repatriated to Pakistan. Further, it was necessary to get the Pakistan territory evacuated from the Indian occupation.

The prisoners-of-war were held in India under the orders of the joint India Bangladesh command. The Geneva Convention on Prisoners of War of 1949 provided that prisoners of war, should be repatriated as soon as possible after the cessation of active hostility. Therefore, India was under moral pressure to release the Pakistani prisoners-of-war. Surrender of Pakistan in Bangladesh was an explosive issue for Bangladesh also for three reasons.

About 4,00,000 Bengalis were detained in Pakistan. This figure included 33,000 armed forces personnel and their families and 75,000 civil servants and their families. There, armed forces personnel were living in concentration camps. They were living in penury and were suffering great mental tension and physical limitation.

Secondly, there were 2,60,000 Pakistanis, called Biharis, still living in Bangladesh. They owed allegiance to Pakistan. Bangladesh wanted to send them to Pakistan, but President ZA Bhutto of Pakistan disowned them.

There was also the third issue of division of assets and liabilities between Pakistan and Bangladesh.

It was in this context that Simla Pact was signed between India and Pakistan on 2 July 1972 in which India got the promise from Pakistan that their differences should be resolved by peaceful means through bilateral negotiations, or by any other peaceful means mutually agreed upon between them. The two countries also committed themselves to respect each other's national unity, territorial integrity, and political independence of each other. This was Pakistani concession to India. In return Pakistan got withdrawal of Indian forces from Pakistan territory.

This treaty thus marked the victory of India in the sense of extracting a promise of non-aggression from Pakistan, for which India was insistent since the birth of Pakistan.

It was also the victory of President ZA Bhutto of Pakistan in having got back the Pakistani territory occupied by India.

The Simla Pact got a favourable response in the public opinion in India. The Jana Sangh however, opposed it. The Jana Sangh charged that India agreed to this pact under Soviet pressure. It charged that the territory exchanged between India and Pakistan was quite unequal. Pakistan returned a small patch of Indian land in Rajasthan as India returned big chunk of Pakistani territory in Sindh and Punjab. Further the Jana Sangh said that taking into account the past background of President ZA Bhutto, he could not be dependent upon to implement the Pact faithfully.

Thus, Atal Bihari Vajpayee, the leader of the Jana Sangh charged that President ZA Bhutto achieved all his three objectives without conceding anything to India. The three objectives achieved by ZA Bhutto were getting back the Pakistani territory which was under Indian occupation.

Secondly, securing the release of 90,000 Pakistani prisoners-of-war and thirdly getting Kashmir issue reopened.

He also said that India failed to get a package agreement with Pakistan, because the Indian Government had itself described the pact as the first step and not the final step.

Dr Bhai Mahavir said that the reference to the "final settlement of Jammu and Kashmir" in the Simla Pact meant negotiation would be started with Pakistan about Kashmir. This would be in contradiction to the repeated assertion of the Indian Government that Kashmir problem was finally settled. The Bharatiya Jana Sangh viewed the Simla Summit as "a great betrayal of the Indian people." It was a tragic blunder. It was another of a series of 'sell out' to Pakistan. The Simla Summit plunged India once again into the abyss of no war no peace statement with Pakistan. The Indian government committed its army to withdraw from the hard-won territories in Punjab and Sindh without first obtaining any commitment from Pakistan on the major issue of discord which had plagued relations between the two nations for twenty-five years, the issue of Kashmir.

It is obvious even to the meanest intelligence that there can be no durable peace with Pakistan unless vexed issue Kashmir is finally and fully settled.[51]

The Jana Sangh opposed the terms of the Simla Agreement and characterized it as 'a sell-out'. Its resolution said

> "The Working Committee of the Bharatiya Jana Sangh is shocked at the way the Prime Minister let down the country in Simla. Its worst fears have come true. The history of Tashkent has been repeated in worse form. What

was won on the battlefield by the blood of the jawans has been bartered away at the negotiating table for a piece of paper. New uncertainties have been created about the long settled issue of Kashmir's accession and Pakistan has been acknowledged as a party. Issues like the vacation of illegal Pak occupation of over 30,000 square miles of Jammu and Kashmir State, arms limitations, recovery of over a thousand crores of long standing dues from Pakistan including Pakistan's share in the public debt of united India, Indian properties confiscated in 1965, compensation for surplus of evacuee property, and expenditure incurred on refugees pushed into India last year were not even broached by Smt Gandhi. It has been a sellout, pure and simple."[52]

According to Jana Sangh, ZA Bhutto came to Simla with three objectives:

(i) Recovery of lost territory,

(ii) Return of Prisoners of War, and

(iii) Reopening of Kashmir issue.

In the view of the Jana Sangh, ZA Bhutto won the first and the third, paved the way for the second which now only awaited Pakistan's recognition of Bangladesh.

The Jana Sangh said that

"The Prime Minister went to the Summit, promising to get a package deal for a durable peace. She has lost on both counts and has wasted a golden opportunity for a mass of verbiage. That a victorious country should have been asked to swallow this insult by its Prime Minister is perhaps the first instance of its kind in world history.

The Pact is being painted as glorious achievement because the two countries have pledged to settle their disputes peacefully through bilateral talks. The Working Committee notes that such expressions of good intentions have characterized all our agreements starting with the Inner Dominion Agreement of December 1948 (when Pakistani's hordes were already ravaging Indian territory in Kashmir), followed by Nehru-Liaquat Pact and ending with the Tashkent Declaration of 1965 each one of which was honoured by Pakistan more in the breach than in observance. The bilateral clause (which has kept a window open for foreign intervention under 'mutually agreed'[53] solutions is already being given different interpretations. While the Prime Minister thinks that Pakistan is bound to keep the Kashmir case out of UNO, President ZA Bhutto hints that nothing prevents him from raising it there again.

The Working Committee believed that by signing the Simla Pact, Smt Indira Gandhi has done great dis-service to the country. Obviously she has succumbed to the pressure of big powers. While America's 'tilt' towards Pakistan is well-known, Russia has been anxious to regain some of its lost good-will in Pakistan, Dhar's dash to Moscow, President Podgorny's inexplicable halt and talks with Swaran Singh in Calcutta, followed by Moscow's reassurance to Pakistan Foreign Secretary Aziz Ahmad, was obvious indicators of Russia's 'advice' that India should be magnanimous. The talk showed all the signs of heading towards a deadlock. That at the very eleventh hours the obstacles mysteriously melted away shows that there is more in it than meets the eye. President ZA Bhutto's prompt and profuse thanks to Russia and America for their help in bringing about the agreement, was not mere diplomatic courtesy."[54]

The Working Committee, therefore, urged upon the President of India not to rectify the agreement till a referendum is carried out to ascertain the people's wishes. It calls upon the people of India to make it clear to the government in uncertain terms that they reject this dishonourable agreement.

Dr Bhai Mahavir charged that ZA Bhutto had succeeded in hoodwinking India. He quoted Bhutto that having won from India the more difficult concession of troops withdrawal, he was confident of securing the early release of Pakistani prisoners-of-war in India as prisoners cannot be kept indefinitely.

Thus, Jana Sangh's attitude on Simla Pact was one of distrusts of Pakistan and criticism of the Government of India, for having being entrapped by Pakistan's promises.

Jana Sangh's Role

During the war, workers of the Jana Sangh, both men and women, made a notable contribution towards maintaining the morale of the people. A countrywide programme was successfully organized for running canteens, reception centres etc for the jawans. In the border areas, our workers assisted the security forces in variety of matters. In Fazilka, even after most civilians had quit the town as a result of constant shelling by the Pakistanis. Jana Sangh workers stayed and saw to it that the blood requirement of the wounded jawans was fully met. They even succeeded in persuading the military authorities not to order a formal evacuation of the town. Similar incident occurred in other parts of the country also. The Jana Sangh support to the war effort was actuated purely by a sense of duty and not by any desire for appreciation or regard.[55]

While the Indo-Pak war was yet on, the Prime Minister, in consultation with leaders of opposition parties, decided to postpone Assembly Elections for one year. A Bill to this effect was prepared and was to be introduced in Parliament. It was argued that as the war had ended, postponing elections would not be well received in the world. This obviously was a flimsy excuse. Truth was that the ruling party was keen to exploit the military victory for political advantage.

Other countries also have fought wars, and have won wars. But the political leadership of no other democratic country has ever sought to convert a national victory into political dividends in an unseemly manner as was done in the Assembly Elections following the Indo-Pak war.

The Assembly elections of 1972 cannot be regarded free and fair. Of course, even in the past there have often been complaints of irregularities right from the stage of preparation of electoral rolls to the counting of votes and declaration of election results. But the kind and scale of practices indulged in this time certainly distorted the entire election's outcome. In various states, voters were physically prevented from exercising their right of franchise. Polling was actually captured by supporters of certain parties. Armed hoodlums terrorized the electors into voting for specific parties or candidates or not voting at all.

At various booths, ballot papers were forcibly stamped by outsiders. At places, the presiding officers actually co-operated in all this and the police either remained indifferent or assisted in this subversion of law. There have been reports of tempering with ballot boxes and of arbitrary decisions taken by returning officers at the counting winning candidates were declared defeated and losing candidates announced as elected.

In this election, governmental machinery has been misused openly and shamelessly. In flagrant violation of democratic practices and established conventions Radio, Television and Films Division were converted into propaganda instruments of the ruling party. The dividing line between the government and the ruling party vanished. Capitalists and industrialists were bribed or bullied into making huge donations to the Congress

Party. A new tactic adopted this time was that these moneyed people were clearly told not to contribute anything to the opposition parties. Jeeps purchased by the Defence Ministry were used for the election Campaign of the Ruling Party. Air force planes and helicopters were freely used. It was thus a very unequal battle which the opposition parties had to fight.

It is highly significant that with all these advantages more voters voted against the Congress than for it. In several states the Congress polled fewer votes than in 1971. In Andhra for instance the Congress poll percentage fell from 55% to 52%, in Maharashtra from 63.8% to 56.62%, in Haryana from 53% to 46.9% and in Delhi from 64% to 48%.

At the Ghaziabad Session I had said that if Pakistan is defeated in a war and an independent Bangladesh is formed, the Jana Sangh should be prepared to lose some seats in the election that would follow. There is no doubt that the Bangladesh happenings had an impact on these elections but the measure of success that has come to the ruling Party. The Congress itself did not expect and could not explain this, solely on the basis of the Bangladesh issue. Fact is that in this year's poll, the ruling party cast all scrapes to the winds and resorted to all kinds of methods to win the elections.

When political parties see nothing wrong in trying to capture political parties, and having captured it once, in trying to perpetuate themselves in office by means, fair or foul, democracy in the country must be considered as being gravely imperilled. It is high time that those who believe in democracy all came together and decided to launch a determined and concerted struggle to ensure that elections in the country are free and fair.

India won the war but this victory cannot be regarded as a guarantee of stable peace. Pakistan's war machine in the West remains, more or less, intact. China and the US continue to supply arms to Pakistan in large quantities. Pakistan is receiving arms also from Jordan, Saudi Arabia, Iran and Turkey who are its military allies. President ZA Bhutto has been talking about making the Pakistani army the finest fighting machine in Asia. A vigorous campaign has been going on in Pakistan for the enrolment of new recruits to the army. Chinese instructors are busy training Pakistanis in the use of new weapons. The notorious General Tikka Khan is now the Chief of Pakistan's armed forces. President ZA Bhutto is very much dependent on the army for his position. The United States as well as China has shown no change yet in their earlier attitudes of using Pakistan as an instrument of their policy in this part of the world. Bhutto needs their military and economic support badly and cannot do without it. The fond hope, therefore, that Pakistan has already learnt a lesson from its 1971 defeat and will readily agree to live henceforth as a good and friendly neighbour to India does not quite fit in with the reality of the situation.

Vajpayee in his Presidential Address at Bhagalpur said in 1972, Pakistan must realize that its dream of becoming a focal point of inspiration for all Muslims in this region of the world lies buried in Dacca, and cannot be revived again. The politics of religion, on the basis of which Pakistan has been staking its claim to Jammu-Kashmir, has also come to an end. So, instead of prattling about self determination for Jammu-Kashmir, ZA Bhutto would do well to get ready to vacate his aggression in that state. India cannot pursuit the aggressor enjoy the fruits of his aggression. Historically the entire Jammu-Kashmir state is an inseparable part of India. The international Boundary between India and Pakistan will be where the boundary of erstwhile Jammu-Kashmir state was in 1947. Those persons and parties who would like the present cease-fire to be accepted as the international boundary with minor adjustments and who are willing to make this the basis of

India's agreement with Pakistan should understand that this would be a betrayal of national integrity and the Indian Constitution. The Indian people will not endorse any attempt to buy dubious friendship with Pakistan at the cost of one-third Kashmir. Kashmir, the Jana Sangh holds, is non-negotiable.[56]

He further said, "Apart from the question of Pakistan's aggression in Kashmir, there are several other matters outstanding between India and Pakistan which must be settled. Pakistan has been holding on to Evacuee property worth ₹1,000 crore. Pakistan also owes to us a pre-partition debt of ₹300 crore. Indian goods illegally confiscated by Pakistan during the 1965 war also are yet to be returned. Adequate war reparations besides must be made to India for the loss in life and property which India has suffered during the 1971 war. We must recover also from Pakistan the amount we have spent on Bangladesh refugees. No peace settlement can be regarded as satisfactory unless it resolves these issues. The Indian people must remain vigilant and see to it that the Government of India does not succumb to any foreign pressure nor is led astray by any wishy-washy talk of friendship into sacrificing vital national interests at the negotiating table.[57]

References

1. Resolution of the Muslim League passed in its Lahore Session on 23, March 1940, as quoted by Syed Sharifuddin Pirzada (Lahore, The All Pakistan Legal Decision, 1963), p 2.
2. Set T Lee Auspitz (*et al*), "History of Economic and Political Domination of East Pakistan", in *Bangladesh Documents* (New Delhi, Publications Division, nd) pp 5-8.
3. President Yahya Khan announcement, 26 March 1969.
4. Anthony Mascarenhas, *The Rape of Bangladesh* (Delhi, Vikas Publication, 1971), p 44.

5. Mascarenhas, *op cit*, p 45.
6. Voting percentage figures given by the Chief Election Commissioner and quoted in *Tribune* (Chandigarh), 7 February 1971.
7. *Organiser* (New Delhi, Vol XXV, No 1, 14 August 1971), p 8.
8. *The Sunday Times*, London, 13 June 1971.
9. *The Times*, 20 December 1971.
10. BJS Party Documents, East Bengal against Pakistan Domination, Vol 3 (Central Office 1973), p 87.
11. *Ibid.*
12. Exodus from East Bengal, Bharatiya Jana Sangh. Party Document 1951-72 Volume 3, Resolutions on Defence, And External Affairs, Vithalbhai Patel Bhavan, New Delhi, 1973, p 23.
13. *Ibid.*
14. *Exodus From East Bengal*, *op cit*, p 37.
15. *Ibid.*
16. *Ibid*, 28 August 1965, Calcutta AIGC, All India General Council.
17. Bharatiya Jana Sangh Party Documents, Vol 3 (New Delhi, Bharatiya Jana Sangh, 1973), p 154.
18. Foreign Policy is neither Rational nor National, Bharatiya Jana Sangh Party Documents, Vol 3, Central Office (New Delhi, 1973), p 156.
19. *Ibid.*
20. Immediate Help to Bangladesh, Udaipur, Vol XVII, All India Session, 2 July 1971.
21. Bangladesh No more within Pakistan, Central Working Committee, 9 October 1971 (71.06).
22. Bharatiya Jana Sangh, Presidential Address, Udaipur Session, 3-4 July 1971.
23. *Ibid.*
24. *Ibid.*
25. *Ibid.*
26. *Ibid.*
27. *Ibid.*
28. *Ibid.*

29. Bharatiya Jana Sangh Party Documents, Vol 3, *op cit*, p 160.
30. Bangladesh No more within Pakistan, *op cit*, p 161.
31. Sangh wants Pindiland for Refugees, *The Indian Express*, 14 July 1970, p 5.
32. Vajpayee's Call, *The Indian Express*, 5 July 1971, p 7.
33. Balraj Madhok, *Ibid*.
34. *Ibid*.
35. Bangladesh (Bharatiya Jana Sangh, Central Office. New Delhi. 1971), p 4.
36. *Ibid*, p 7.
37. *Ibid*, p 11.
38. Bharatiya Jana Sangh. Resolution on Bangladesh, 3-4 July 1971, Udaipur.
39. *Ibid*.
40. *Ibid*.
41. Resolution No 71.66, 9 October 1971, Madras CWC, *Ibid*, pp 159-161.
42. *Ibid*.
43. Resolution No 71.08, National Security No v. 272972, Ghaziabad, Bharatiya Jana Sangh Party Documents, Vol III (New Delhi, India).
44. Bharatiya Jana Sangh, Resolution passed by the Bharatiya Pratinidhi Sabha Session, Udaipur, 3-4 July 1971 (Delhi, Navchetan Press 1971) pp 8-9.
45. *Ibid*, p 42.
46. Indira-Vajpayee Correspondence, "Dragging Mazib to Mahil, Jana Sangh" (New Delhi, Bharatiya Jana Sangh, nd), p 2.
47. Bharatiya Jana Sangh, Party Documents 1951-72, Vol 3, Resolution on Defence and External Affairs (New Delhi, 1973), p 15.
48. *Ibid*.
49. Central Working Committee, Bharatiya Jana Sangh, 27, January 1972, Bhopal.
50. Bharatiya Jana Sangh, *Simla Surrender* (Delhi, Navchetan Press, 1972), p 1. Atal Bihari Vajpayee, *Simla Samjhauta* (New Delhi, Bharatiya Jana Sangh Publication, 1972), pp 13-14.

51. *Simla Surrender*, Bharatiya Jana Sangh Publication, Naya Bazar, Delhi, nd.
52. *Ibid.*
53. *Ibid.*
54. Bharatiya Jana Sangh, Presidential Address, Atal Bihari Vajpayee, Bhagalpur, 5-7 May 1972.
55. Bharatiya Jana Sangh, Presidential Address, Bhagalpur, 5-7 May 1972
56. *Ibid.*
57. *Ibid.*

CHAPTER 7

Bharatiya Janata Party Governments at Centre

1996 Government of Atal Bihari Vajpayee

Following victories in several State elections and better performance in General Election in 1996, Bharatiya Janata Party (BJP) won 161 Lok Sabha seats, making it the largest party in parliament. Atal Bihari Vajpayee was sworn in as Prime Minister, but was unable to attain a majority in the Lok Sabha, forcing the government to resign after 13 days. A coalition of regional parties formed the government, but this coalition was short-lived, and mid-term polls were held in 1998.

1998 Government of Atal Bihari Vajpayee

BJP contested the 1998 General Election, leading a coalition called National Democratic Alliance (NDA), which contained its existing allies like the Samata Party, Shiromani Akali Dal, Shiv Sena, All India Anna Dravida Munnetra Kazhagam (AIADMK) and the Biju Janata Dal (BJD). Among these regional parties, Shiv Sena was the only party which had an ideology similar to the BJP. The NDA had a majority with outside support of Telugu Desam Party (TDP) and Atal Bihari Vajpayee returned as Prime Minister. However, the coalition ruptured in May 1999 when Jayalalitha, leader of AIADMK, withdrew her support, and fresh elections were held again in 1999.

1999-2004 Government of Atal Bihari Vajpayee

On 13 October 1999, NDA, without AIADMK, won 303 seats in Parliament, an outright majority. Atal Bihari Vajpayee became Prime Minister for the third time; Lal Krishna Advani became Deputy Prime Minister and Home Minister. This NDA government lasted its full term of 5 years. Its policy agenda included a more aggressive stance on defence and terror as well as neo-liberal economic policies.

Major Achievements of Vajpayee Government

1. He took strategically extremely important and a courageous decision in May 1998 to make India a nuclear power and conducted nuclear tests even in the face of opposition of several world powers. Under his leadership, India successfully overcame sanctions imposed by certain big powers.
2. He made earnest efforts to normalise relations with Pakistan, beginning with his historic Bus Yatra to Lahore in February 1999. However, when Pakistan betrayed his trust, India's armed forces, under his leadership, defeated Pakistan in the Kargil war in 1999.
3. His government undertook the most comprehensive review of the system of managing India's national security (both external and internal) and initiated corrective measures. This included firm measures to combat cross-border terrorism sponsored by Pakistan. The combination of his strong security policy and farsighted foreign policy forced Islamabad to commit for the first time (in January 2004) that Pakistan would not allow its soil (or territory controlled by it) to be used for terrorist activities against India. Under the NDA regime, for the first time, a separate Border Management Department was established and a Defence Intelligence Unit created.

4. He made sincere and successful efforts to marginalise militancy and separatism in Jammu and Kashmir (J&K) and bring peace and normalcy in the State. Under his leadership of the central government, free and fair elections were held in J&K for the first time after many decades.
5. He unveiled the National Highway Development Project (NHDP) to construct world-class highways in India, connecting four metros (Golden Quadrilateral) and also the four corners of the country through the north-south and east-west corridors. NHDP is the most ambitious infrastructure project since India's independence, and also the greatest road construction project after the Grand Trunk Road (from Kolkata to Kabul), which was initiated by the Maurya empire in the 3rd century BC and renovated by Sher Shah Suri in the 16th century.
6. He also initiated the Pradhan Mantri Gram Sadak Yojana (PMGSY), with the goal of connecting all the villages and hamlets in India with good all-weather roads. It is the largest project in rural connectivity since independence.
7. Besides physical connectivity, his government took bold steps to build digital connectivity in the country. It ushered in a reform-oriented telecom and IT policies which boosted mobile and internet services in India and also helped make India a 'software superpower'. He is also the architect of the pioneering efforts towards exploring the possibility of linking rivers for which, he established a dedicated working group.
8. His government started the Sarva Shiksha Abhiyan, which is India's flagship programme for achievement of universalisation of Elementary Education.
9. Harmony remains the hallmark of the good governance regime of Atal Bihari Vajpayee. As Prime Minister, he ensured harmonious relations between the Centre and the

States through a carefully cultivated mutuality of confidence. This stands in stark contrast to the approach of the Congress or Congress-led governments at the Centre frequently inviting fairly substantiated allegations of discriminatory approach towards State governments run by opposition parties.

10. He not only coined the phrase 'Coalition Dharma' (proper ethos to conduct coalition politics in a cohesive manner, with commitment to an agreed programme, and in an atmosphere of mutual trust and understanding among alliance partners) but also left behind an exemplary model of how to practise it. He thereby greatly strengthened the emergence of bi-polarity in Indian polity through cultivation of healthy inter-personal and inter-party relationships.
11. Under his leadership, India promoted friendship and cooperation with all the major countries in the world, especially in the immediate neighbourhood. India's relations with USA and other Western nations became deeper and broader. Our traditionally friendly relations with Russia became stronger. Besides promoting mutually beneficial economic ties between India and China, his government also initiated a structured mechanism for high-level dialogue to resolve the border dispute between the two countries. Besides elevating India's relations with Japan to a strategic level, he gave a new impetus to India's 'Look East Policy' to build closer ties with countries in South-East Asia and East Asia.

    All these forward-looking foreign policy initiatives, combined with Vajpayee's visionary steps to strengthen India's national security and development, contributed to an immense rise in India's global profile and prestige.

Besides all these, Atal Bihari Vajpayee Government at the centre needs to be credited for creation of new departments like Ministry of Tribal Affairs, Department of North-East Region and converting the Social Welfare Ministry into the Ministry of Social Justice. Besides, under his leadership; for the first time in the post-independence history of India, the process of long overdue creation of three new small States—Uttarakhand, Chhattisgarh and Jharkhand—was taken to its logical end through, what can be described as Politics of Consensus. Besides, it was under his regime that both the houses of Parliament had a joint historic session to pass the Prevention Of Terrorism Act (POTA) and thereby give a strong signal to anti-national forces. He had a remarkable ability to reach out to those who were otherwise known for being stubborn and unrelenting. In border areas like Nagaland and J&K he touched the hearts of the people while touring the respective States and that added immensely to the strength of the peace processes in both these States.

On 25 December 2014, President of India announced the Bharat Ratna, India's highest civilian honour, to Atal Bihari Vajpayee. In a special gesture, President Pranab Mukherjee conferred Bharat Ratna to Atal Bihari Vajpayee in his residence on 27 March 2015. His birthday, 25 December, was declared 'Good Governance Day'.

2014 Narendra Modi Government

When the history of 2014 general election will be written, one thing that will stand out is the historic campaign undertaken by Narendra Modi to reach out to the people of India in order to convey the message of development and good governance. Never before in India's electoral history has a leader emerged as such a bright ray of hope for people. Never before has a campaign been undertaken with so much innovation and precision.

It would not be an exaggeration to describe the Modi campaign as one of the biggest mass mobilisation exercise seen anywhere in the history of electioneering. The scale and intensity of the campaign becomes even bigger when one understands the large population and geographic spread of India. In the past, political leaders have led marathon campaigns but the scale at which this campaign was done beats them all by miles!

Starting from 15th September 2013, when Narendra Modi addressed his 1st rally after being anointed as the BJP's PM candidate till 10th May 2014 when campaigning for the last phase of 2014 General Election ends, Narendra Modi would have addressed 437 historic rallies across India from J&K to Kanyakumari, from Amreli to Arunachal Pradesh. From 15th March to 10th May he would have travelled almost 3 lakh kilometres! Add to the 1,350 rallies through 3-D technology across the nation.

India voted overwhelmingly in favour of Narendra Modi, giving him a clear majority and a massive mandate in the 2014 General Elections for a regime change. NDA which comprises BJP and 24 smaller parties bagged 336 seats. At the height of its popularity during Atal Bihari Vajpayee regime, considered to be the tallest leader of the party, BJP got 182 seats in 1998 and 1999, in the backdrop of Ayodhya movement and the Rath Yatra undertaken by Lal Krishna Advani. Led by Narendra Modi in 2014, BJP won the General Election with 282 seats. Narendra Modi—BJP's campaign leader and prime ministerial candidate, won from both the constituencies—Vadodara (Gujarat) and Varanasi (Uttar Pradesh).

This was the biggest victory since the 1984 election that Rajiv Gandhi won with 414 Lok Sabha seats. It is also the first time ever in the 67-year history of independent India that a non-Congress party has won a simple majority.

Congress was handed its worst-ever defeat with only 46 MPs in parliament. Sonia Gandhi and Rahul Gandhi were the only 2 Congress candidates to win in Uttar Pradesh. BJP's strongest performance came from Uttar Pradesh, where BJP won 72 out of 80 seats. One seat was won by BJP ally Apna Dal. In 2009 BJP won only 10 seats in Uttar Pradesh. Bahujan Samaj Party (BSP) of Mayawati failed to open its account. Samajwadi Party (SP) won only 5 seats—members of Mulayam Singh Yadav's family.

Swearing-in Ceremony of Narendra Modi

Post the declaration of election results on 16 May 2014, Modi met the President of India Pranab Mukherjee on 20th May where President Mukherjee invited him to form the new government. Bharatiya Janata Party announced that Narendra Modi will be sworn in on 26th May 2014 at the forecourts of the Rashtrapati Bhavan as the 15th Prime Minister of India.

On 26th May 2014, Prime Minister-designate Narendra Modi took oath at the Rashtrapati Bhavan at 6 PM as the 15th Prime Minister of India along with his Cabinet. Around 3,500 Indian and foreign dignitaries attended the ceremony, including leaders from all the seven SAARC nations. Outgoing Prime Minister Manmohan Singh, former Presidents—Abdul Kalam and Pratibha Patil, Vice-President Hamid Ansari, Congress President Sonia Gandhi were among those who participated in the oath-taking ceremony. The following SAARC heads of government attended the ceremony: (1) Hamid Karzai, President of Afghanistan; (2) Shirin Sharmin Chaudhury, Speaker of Jatiyo Sangshad (House of the Nation), Bangladesh, accepted the invitation on behalf of the Prime Minister Sheikh Hasina as she had a pre-planned visit to Japan; (3) Tshering Tobgay, Prime Minister of Bhutan; (4) Abdulla Yameen Abdul Gayoom, President of Maldives; (5) Navin Ramgoolam, Prime Minister of Mauritius; (6) Sushil Koirala, Prime Minister of Nepal; (7) Nawaz Sharif, Prime Minister of Pakistan; and (8) Mahinda Rajapaksa, President of Sri Lanka.

Major Initiatives of Narendra Modi Government

1. In the very initial months of NDA Government, it took up the task of providing toilets in all schools.
2. NDA implemented the Jana Dhan Yojana and opened more than 19 crore bank accounts for financial inclusion. So far, banks have collected more than 27,696 crore rupees from Jana Dhan Yojana depositors.
3. PaHaL or Pratyaksha Hastaantarit Laabh, formerly the Direct Benefit Transfer Scheme for LPG subsidy, is a Direct Benefit Transfer scheme for liquefied petroleum gas (LPG) subsidy in India. Under the scheme, LPG cylinders are sold at market rates and consumers receive a subsidy from the Union Government directly into their bank accounts. It replaced the previous system of selling subsidised LPG cylinders directly to consumers. It is the largest cash transfer programme in the world. Up to 13 August 2015, 13.9 crore LPG consumers are enrolled under the scheme.
4. NDA launched MUDRA Bank for financing 6 crore small vendors and businesses, 61% of whom are SCs, STs, OBCs and Minorities. Under the Pradhan Mantri Mudra Yojana, banks have disbursed Rs. 45,948.28 crore as on November 2015 which has benefited 66 lakh borrowers.
5. NDA launched Pradhan Mantri Krishi Sinchai Yojana which the Congress did not think of in 60 years.
6. NDA planned to see that by 2022, no family remains without roof over its head.
7. The Soil Health Card scheme has been launched to enhance farm productivity and reduce expenses, thereby enhancing the farmer's income.
8. NDA came out with a comprehensive social security scheme for the poor and marginalised, old and those with low-income levels.

9. Swachh Bharat Mission has been started to see that health and hygiene issues of the poor, do not affect the working capacity and output of the poor and labourers.
10. Indian Railways, on which the common man travels, is being changed for the better.
11. NDA have set up Skill Development Ministry to enhance employability of the youth to whom we are committed to provide jobs through initiatives like 'Make in India'. In the past, the country had been led into an economy of jobless growth.
12. NDA provided for reservation of women in the police forces of Union Territories. This was done even when there were no elections around the corner.
13. Through the regime of coal auction that NDA have put in place, more than 3 lakh crore rupees have already been generated for the less-developed States of India. This money will be used for the poor of those states.

Narendra Modi's International Visits

As of December 2015, Narendra Modi has made 33 foreign trips which includes USA and countries of Europe and Asia. Visits to USA were also to attend United Nations General Assembly meetings. A few of the foreign visits were State visits to Asian countries, following his neighbourhood first and act east policies.

Benefits of Narendra Modi's Foreign Relations

- US-India Business Council (USIBC) announced investments worth $41 billion into India in the next 3 years.
- US President Barack Obama announced $4 billion in government-backed investments and lending to India.
- Prime Minister Narendra Modi convinced USA to drop rule of nuclear fuel tracking and sorted out liabilities rules which now open the gates for next 16 nuclear power plant projects.

- President Francois Hollande of France supports India's permanent membership of UN Security Council.
- President Hollande announced that France will invest 2 billion euros in India.
- Modi's 'Make in India' dream takes off with Airbus outsourcing pledge for $2 billion.
- France will help in the development of three smart cities in India, including Pondicherry and Nagpur.
- French National Railways agreed to co-finance an execution study for a semi-high speed project on upgradation of the Delhi-Chandigarh line to 200 kmph.
- Prime Minister Narendra Modi renegotiated Rafale fighter Jets deal with France personally and bought 36 Jets on ASAP basis.
- Prime Minister Narendra Modi was able to convince France to make nuclear reactors with the latest technology in India on 'Make in India' efforts, with collaboration with an Indian company as a partner.
- Canada agreed to supply 3,000 metric tonnes of uranium to India for its civil nuclear plants for next 5 years.
- The Japanese Prime Minister Shinzo Abe committed $35 billion in public and private investment and financing for the next five years. Japan committed $12 billion loan at negligible interest for 'Bullet Train' and another $12 billion for 'Make in India' initiative, besides inking far-reaching pacts on defence and nuclear energy.
- Recognising the new initiatives of Prime Minister Narendra Modi to facilitate trade and investment, encourage the investment institutions of UAE to raise their investments in India, including through the establishment of UAE-India Infrastructure Investment Fund, with the aim of reaching a target of $75 billion to support investment in India's plans for rapid expansion of next generation infrastructure,

especially in railways, ports, roads, airports and industrial corridors and parks.

- Chinese President Xi Jinping committed $20 billion investment in India.
- India managed to bring back 4,500+ Indians from war zone in Yemen and also brought foreign nationals of 41 different countries, which put India's name onto the highest platform globally in conducting this rescue mission.

In 57 years' rule, Congress could not get 'Achche Din' and now Congress wants 'Achche Din' in just 18 months. Such a shameful double standard thinking. People of India elected a Prime Minister not a magician.

Narendra Modi on Corruption

Asserting that his government is very strict in punishing the corrupt, Prime Minister Narendra Modi said that 45 senior officers have either been removed or faced pension cuts for 'unsatisfactory performance and delivery in public service'.

> "We have also introduced a provision under the Prevention of Money Laundering Act for restitution of assets. This will enable millions of poor investors who have lost money in ponzi schemes to recover a part of their hard earned money."

"India has zero tolerance on black money and corruption," Prime Minister Narendra Modi said at the G20 Summit while seeking greater global cooperation for return of illicit money stashed abroad.

> "We need greater international cooperation for return of illicit money to the country of origin. We must address the barriers of excessive banking secrecy, and complex legal and regulatory frameworks. My government has zero tolerance on corruption and black money. We have enacted a new law to deal with undisclosed assets and income kept abroad."

Narendra Modi on Terrorism

Prime Minister Narendra Modi said India has a 'difficult neighbourhood', and that several countries have reached out to India to deal with the rising threat of terrorism and radicalisation across regions 'including the Islamic world'.

In an oblique reference to Pakistan for using terrorism as an instrument of state policy, Prime Minister Narendra Modi pushed for the adoption of a Comprehensive Convention on International Terrorism 'without any delay' at the G-20 summit.

> "Terrorism is a principle global challenge.... Old structures of terrorism remain. There are countries that stili use it as an instrument of State policy.... There should be no distinction between terrorist groups or discrimination between states.... We need to delink terror and religion and work together to counter radicalisation."

Prime Minister Narendra Modi urged the world to speak in one voice against terrorism and said that countries must be held accountable for sanctuaries and support to terror.

> "Terrorism does not just take a toll on lives, but can derail economies.... We must delink terrorism from religion and assert the human value that defines every faith."

Are you with terrorism or against it? Prime Minister Modi asks in Dubai.

> "We have spoken in one voice against terrorism, ... those who can understand will understand.... We are victims of terrorism for 40 years. Many innocent people have lost their lives. Those who indulge in terrorism must be punished.... Good terrorist, bad terrorist, good Taliban, bad Taliban, this won't work. A decision has to be taken: Are you with terrorism or humanity?"

Voicing concern over a spate of recent terror attacks in several countries, Prime Minister Narendra Modi said in his remarks at the East Asia Summit in Kuala Lumpur:

> "We often thought of terrorism as a peripheral problem for this region. The barbaric terrorist strikes in Paris, Ankara, Beirut, Mali and on the Russian aircraft is a stark reminder that its shadow stretches across our societies and our world, both in recruitment and choice of targets.... There is no distinction between groups. There are no sanctuaries. There are no funds. There is no access to arms. But, we also have to work within our societies and with our youth."

Narendra Modi on Challenges of Climate Change

> "Climate change is a major global challenge. But it is not of our making. It is the result of global warming that came from prosperity and progress of an industrial age powered by fossil fuel."

Prime Minister Narendra Modi delivered a stern message to affluent nations, saying 'those with luxury of choices' should sharply reduce emissions. Prime Minister Modi's comments came on the sidelines of a high-stake United Nations Conference in Paris where over 150 world leaders have gathered in a bid to nail down a pact to limit global warming amid deep divisions between rich and poor countries. Modi said while inaugurating the India pavilion at the Paris summit, toughening his country's stand in the face of recent US criticism of India.

> "But we in India face consequences. We see the risk to our farmers. We are concerned about rising oceans that threaten our 7,500 km of coastline and 1,300 islands. We worry about the glaciers that feed our rivers and nurture our civilisation."

Modi said India wants a 'comprehensive equitable and durable agreement'.

> "India's progress is our destiny and right of our people. But we must also lead in combating climate change.... We need a genuine global partnership. Democratic India must grow rapidly to meet energy needs of everyone.... We assume advanced nations will take ambitious targets. It's not a question of historical responsibility. They also have room for emission cuts. Climate justice demands with lethal carbon space, developing countries must have enough room to grow."

"We can achieve the same level of development, prosperity and well-being without necessarily going down the path of reckless consumption," Modi told the United Nations General Assembly.

> "It doesn't mean that economies will suffer; it will mean that our economies will take on a different character. For us in India, respect for nature is an integral part of spiritualism. We treat nature's bounties as sacred. Yoga is an invaluable gift of our ancient tradition. Yoga embodies unity of mind and body; thought and action; restraint and fulfilment; harmony between man and nature; a holistic approach to health and well-being. It is not about exercise but to discover the sense of oneness with yourself, the world and the nature. By changing our lifestyle and creating consciousness, it can help us deal with climate change. Let us work towards adopting an International Yoga Day."

Modi's goal was realized on 21st June 2015, when the first International Yoga Day was held.

Article 370

Article 370 of the Indian Constitution is an article that grants special autonomous status to the State of Jammu and Kashmir. The Article is drafted in Part XXI of the Constitution, which relates to Temporary, Transitional and Special Provisions.

Parliamentary Affairs Minister M. Venkaiah Naidu said,

> "There is no change in the BJP's stand on repealing Article 370 of the Constitution, which guarantees special status to Jammu and Kashmir. Repealing Article 370 required a two-third majority in Parliament as the Constitution would have to be amended."

BJP national spokesman Sambit Patra said,

> "As far as the abrogation of Article 370 is concerned, it continues to be part of the core ideology of BJP, but right now we don't have enough numbers in Parliament to do away with it ... but in future when we have the required numbers we will work towards its removal."

In October 2015, a bench of the J&K High Court observed,

> "(The) Article 370, notwithstanding its title 'temporary provision' is a permanent provision of the Constitution. It cannot be abrogated, repealed or even amended as mechanism provided under Clause (3) of Article 370 is no more available.... No other provision of the Constitution as provided under Article 370(1), would be applicable to the State except, by Presidential order in consultation with the State in case the provision is akin to subjects delineated in Instrument of Accession and with concurrence of the State, in case it does not fall within ambit of Instrument of Accession."

Union Minister Jitendra Singh said,

> "BJP has not abandoned its stand on Article 370.... We had grown up in politics understanding the ideology of Dr Syama Prasad Mookerjee, who favoured *'ek nishan, ek vidhan, ek pradhan'* (one flag, one Constitution, one leader).... BJP as a party stands by all ideological principles it has espoused since its creation, wherever there is a coalition, the agenda is based on mutual acceptance.... The government favoured return of Kashmiri Pandits to the Valley with 'respect and security' as it was 'incomplete' without them.... "

Demise of J&K CM Mufti Mohammad Sayeed

Mufti Mohammad Sayeed died on 7th January 2016 at AIIMS (Delhi) due to multiple organ failure. He joined Rajiv Gandhi government in 1986 as Minister of Tourism. He was Home Minister in VP Singh's National Front government. His short stint (1989-90) was marred by the kidnapping of his daughter Rubaiyya Sayeed by Kashmiri militants. He founded People's Democratic Party (PDP) in July 1999. He served twice as the Chief Minister of Jammu and Kashmir. Following a coalition agreement between the BJP and the PDP, Sayeed undertook a second tenure as Chief Minister of the State on 1st March 2015. On 7th November 2015 Prime Minister Narendra Modi announced a package of ₹ 80,000 crore to build Jammu and Kashmir a modern, progressive and prosperous State. On this occasion Narendra Modi said,

> "I will like to follow the three mantras of former Prime Minister Atal Bihari Vajpayee—Kashmiriyat, Jamhooriyat aur Insaniyat (Kashmiri culture, democracy and humanity) —which are the pillars of development of Kashmir."

As the BJP has left it to the PDP to select its Chief Ministerial candidate, decks have been cleared for Mehbooba Mufti (member of Lok Sabha from Anantnag) to become the first woman Chief Minister of Jammu and Kashmir. On 9th January 2016, President Pranab Mukherjee cleared Governor's Rule in Jammu and Kashmir State on the recommendation of Governor NN Vohra.

CHAPTER 8

Conclusion

The BJS was created as a political party with its own distinct ideology. Its ideology was based on what it called the Bharatiya Sanskriti and Maryada. In its amplification, it meant belief on one nation and one culture; faith in Akhand Bharat was but the natural corollary of this belief. And it tried to present solution of all contemporary problems in the light of the basic ideology. Its attitude on the issues confronting India's foreign policy was also coloured and conditioned by its commitment to its ideology.

Pakistan naturally occupied a position of predominant importance in the scheme of things projected by the Jana Sangh, Pakistan stood as a symbol of repudiation and a source of constant provocation and also challenged to the ideology of Akhand Bharat upheld by the Jana Sangh.

Naturally Jana Sangh exhibited an attitude of intense hostility towards Pakistan. This attitude has remained the most important factor and Jana Sangh's attitude on their issues has been determined by this factor. Thus Jana Sangh has been prepared to oppose all those forces which tended to extend sympathy and support to Pakistan and it was prepared to support all those forces which tended to oppose Pakistan. It is practising the simple dictum of Kautiliya and enemy's enemy is the natural friend and enemy's friend is the potential enemy.

Jana Sangh perceived the basic national interest of India related to Pakistan. It was to weaken and oppose Pakistan and for this Jana Sangh was prepared to compromise with any principle or tactics. Principles could be sacrificed for the sake of the interest of nation, but a nation cannot be sacrificed for the sake of principle.

Jana Sangh's attitude towards the three major issues confronting India's foreign policy, that is, Kashmir question. The Arab-Israel conflict and the Bangladesh issue were but an extension of its attitude towards Pakistan.

Jana Sangh has advocated a complete integration of the state of Jammu-Kashmir with India. It criticized the decision for a ceasefire accomplished in 1948; it criticized the promulgation of a separate constitution for the state because it had an unsettling effect in the minds of the people about the finality of the relations of the state with India. It criticized the Tashkent Pact, because under this pact the *status auo* had to be restored there by obliging India to return some chunks of territory which are under the legal occupation of Pakistan. Jana Sangh also criticized the Simla Pact on the same ground.

Jana Sangh advocated a line of action which would have forced Pakistan to vacate that part of the territory of the state which is under its illegal occupation.

Jana Sangh thinks that Pakistan is an unnatural state and it cannot survive except by seeking issues of conflict with India. In this way Kashmir is not the cause of Indo-Pakistan conflict rather it is the result and the symbol of that conflict.

Therefore, Jana Sangh has advocated an attitude of reciprocity towards Pakistan and renunciation of an attitude of, what it calls, appeasement, which it thinks that India has been following all these years. Jana Sangh's attitude regarding the Arab-Israel conflict was also an intention of its pre-occupation with Pakistan. Jana Sangh has neither been anti-Arab nor Pro-Israel. It has advocated peaceful and just solution of the problem which involves right of existence for the state of Israel and right of settlement to the Arab refugees in their own land. It also involves withdrawal of Israel from the Arab territory it occupied by force of arms during three wars.

The Jana Sangh Working Committee had passed resolution to this effect at its meeting in Simla in June-July 1967.

The resolution said that, the Arab countries must relinquish all intentions to destroy Israel and they should gracefully acknowledge its existence and developmental relations with it. At the same time Israel also must co-operate on a large scale for the resettlement of the Arab refugees, who were uprooted from their houses as a result of the establishment of Israel. The solution of the Arab refugees' problem will go long way in the pacification of the situation because in the view of the Jana Sangh,

> "The miserable plight of refugees is a permanent cause for the tension and bitterness subsisting between the Arab and Jews, and it has to be remedied."

Jana Sangh also admonished Israel for its West-oriented attitude and said that Israel must realize that it is basically an Afro-Asian state and so instead of allowing itself to be used just as an instrument of Western diplomacy in West Asia it should play a respectable and purposeful role. It called for right of unrestricted passage for the ships of all nations through the Suez Canal and Gulf of Aquaba though the United Arab Republic should have the right of toll from the passing ships.

Jana Sangh has criticized India's unilateral friendship and solicitude for the Arab nations and India's attitude of touch-me-not with regard to Israel. Jana Sangh has pointed out that Israel has supported India several times in the United Nations where as the Arab nations have opposed India and supported Pakistan on all crucial issues in the UN as well as outside. Even the UAR has not come out openly on the side of India and it has seen nothing wrong in keeping friendly relations with India on the one hand and India's enemies Pakistan and Communist China on the other hand. There has been a tendency on the part of the Arab nations to take India for granted and be indifferent to India's sensitivities.

Jana Sangh called for a policy of reciprocity also with regard to Israel and the Arab nations. On the question of Bangladesh, Jana Sangh saw an opportunity of weakening and dismembering Pakistan. This fitted admirably to the Jana Sangh's own frame of thinking. Naturally, Jana Sangh supported whole-heartedly the liberation movement in Bangladesh. In 1970-71, it demanded early recognition of Bangladesh and when the Government of India extended recognition and an armed conflagration took place between India and Pakistan in December 1971, Jana Sangh was the happiest party and it extended most enthusiastic and vociferous support to the measures adopted by the Government of India. Jana Sangh adopted a secularist attitude, because that was the answer to Pakistan's communalism.

Jana Sangh has considered that the touchstone of the success of the foreign policy of any nation is its capacity to protect and promote the enlightened self-interest of a nation. According to it, the foreign policy pursued by the Congress government in India was a failure. Jana Sangh advocated that India's foreign policy should be re-oriented to make it most realistic, dynamic and firm so that while effectively safeguarding India's interests it may contribute to world peace by upholding the freedom of nations and rights of men. It also advocated a true policy of non-involvement in international tangles and a policy of reciprocity towards Pakistan till such time that it exists as a separate state.

Jana Sangh's attitude on foreign policy matters is thus determined by its ideology.

The BJP remained out of power till the Vajpayee government was formed in 1998. However this government could not continue for long period. It fell down after 13 days due to lack of majority support on the floor of Lok Sabha. The next election was held in 1999 when the BJP and its alliances (NDA) got absolute majority. The President of India once again called Atal Bihari Vajpayee, the leader of the NDA to form a government. He took oath as the Prime Minister of India in the month of November. Thus, the people of India expressed their complete faith in the leadership of Vajpayee who was the most seasoned politician of the country. The Government of India under the leadership of Vajpayee was fully-determined to make India a powerful nation. He knew well that to achieve and avail the prestige in the world politics the country must have notable strength. He realized India must possess atomic energy breaking up the monopoly of the powerful nuclear nations like USA, Great Britain, France, China and Japan. When he became the Prime Minister of India he managed to explode two atom bombs underground at Pokharan to test atomic energy to go for further research in the field of atomic energy. Two experiments were made—first on 11th May 1999, where three explosion made and second on 13.05.1999 where two resolution were made. It made the USA unhappy. As a result that USA banned the supply of uranium to India. It also launched economic action against India. The government of Vajpayee faced bravely the steps taken by the USA. It was such a daring step of NDA government that it could attract the attention of the world. The countries possessing atomic energies opposed such daring step of India, but the Vajpayee led NDA government could hardly give attention to the opposition. This made India, a country possessing atomic energy, adding to its prestige and reputation. Vajpayee thereafter became very popular leader both inside and outside the country.

Vajpayee also adopted various steps to improve the relations between India and Pakistan. He wanted to maintain good relationship with neighbouring countries, by opening the bus route between India and Pakistan. He approved the Samjhauta Express. He himself went to Pakistan after inauguration of the bus. He also invited the President of Pakistan General Musharraf to have dialogue at New Delhi. He came to India where warm welcome was given. Unfortunately, the summit meeting between the chiefs of India and Pakistan did not produce expected fruits due to cunningness of General Musharraf. He started undeclared Kargil war. However, armed forces fought the war with great zeal and bravery; as a result, Pakistani forces were forced to return back evacuating the Indian territory in Kargil.

Atal Bihari Vajpayee, being the leader of BJP-led NDA and the Prime Minister of India had the capability to keep the allies of NDA united. Reverse circumstances appeared several times when the regional leaders—Mamta Banerjee of Bengal, Mayawati of Uttar Pradesh and Jayalalitha of Tamil Nadu—joined the NDA government for sharing power, created problems several times for the Vajpayee government, but Vajpayee had the guts to solve the problems, taking them in good account. Occasions appeared when it seemed that the NDA government will not complete its full tenure, but it was the wisdom of Vajpayee that kept the mentors of the NDA united and work for the betterment of India and its people.

Some have really remarked that Vajpayee was a lotus that has blossomed in the mud. After the exit of Pandit Jawaharlal Nehru from the scene of Indian politics and demise of Indira Gandhi and her son Rajiv Gandhi, it was believed that the era of political dominance of Nehru dynasty was over and in the new political horizon the scope for the Prime Minister out of the Nehru family was bright. At this circumstance it was expected that Vajpayee being the Prime Minister of the country would definitely give last blow to finish the dominance of Nehru's family over politics. Shri Bhandari, in praise of Vajpayee maintained that

> "He (Vajpayee) made a profound impression upon my mind as sensitive, warm, gentle, balanced and thoughtful person—qualities which should help a prime minister."

A critical study of Vajpayee's regime of rule clearly indicates that it is very much difficult to manage and control a coalition government. However, it also shows that a leader like Vajpayee may manage the affairs having patience, wisdom, foresight and broad-mindedness. It was the character and wisdom of Vajpayee that had broadened political base not only for him but for his party also. It was Vajpayee who taught the people how to run a coalition government, and how to utilize the regional forces for betterment of the country. He ruled the country from 1999 to 2004 without many hindrances only because of his liberal attitude and approach. Had there been any other BJP leader to be the Prime Minister it would have been impossible to run the affairs and keep the regional mentors united.

Since Vajpayee had strong faith in his cabinet-colleagues, his government worked hard for development of India and for the enhancement of India's prestige in foreign countries. During his regime some decisive step were taken to normalize relations between India and Pakistan. BJP government wanted to make India a powerful Nation, and for that experiment in the field of atomic energy was must. Hence when the BJP came in power, the NDA government went for experiment of atomic energy blast for that the world became suspicious to India's strength and mission. He took up a number of steps to improve relations with Pakistan. That is why he made the historic Lahore journey and tried best to convince rulers of Pakistan that peace was very essential for both India and Pakistan. That is another fact that Pakistan responded negatively and exposed its heinous crime by starting Kargil war.

The government of Vajpayee completed full tenure. The government of NDA did a number of notable works to improve a lot of the country and its people. The greatest success of Vajpayee as a Prime Minister was that he successfully maintained the unity of coalition government despite various pressures and pools. In the General Election held in 2004, BJP could not secure majority to form the government. This time the UPA under the leadership of Congress secured the required majority to form the government. The basic cause of defeat of the NDA was disunity among coalition partners and weakening strength of the BJP. The party failed to fulfill the desires and needs of the people. In the next general election held in 2009, BJP once again lost the majority support.

The BJP got opportunity to form government at the Centre after ten years in 2014 when sixteenth general elections for the formation of Lok Sabha were held. Surprisingly enough the Party alone secured 284 and its total seats along with alliances (NDA) reached to 334. It means the BJP crossed the magical figure of 272. It all happened due to dashing leadership of Narendra Damodardas Modi who was installed as the would-be Prime Minister of India. He has charismatic character. He tried his best to influence the voters all over the country. The other leaders of the BJP expressed full faith in Modi's qualities and abilities.

Modi was invited to form the government by President Pranab Mukherjee. In the presence of thousands of people, Narendra Modi took oath as Prime Minister of India along with other colleagues on 26 May 2014. The leaders of SAARC countries were respectfully invited to witness the oath ceremony of Modi and his ministers. Almost all the chiefs of SAARC nations accepted the invitation and made themselves available to attend the ceremony. It added the beauty and prestige of India in the field of international politics. Soon after taking oath Narendra Modi assured the people of India to bring back good days for the people. He promised to work hard and sincerely. On the other hand, the people of India have great expectations from the BJP. BJP as a political party emerged as a most powerful national political party. It is expected that the country would get all-round development under the leaders of the BJP and its alliances. The main challenges before the Modi government are to control rising prices all over the country, eradicate corruption and make provisions for the employment of youth. It has to maintain the national integrity.

It is also notable that Atal Bihari Vajpayee, while participating in the BRICS meeting at Brazil, craned reputation for India. He attracted attention of the members of the participating countries including China. He impressed upon the participating members to strengthen the unity of BRICS by having strong economic and political ties as well as integration. Under the persuasion of Atal Bihari Vajpayee, members agreed to establish a bank with sufficient funds in China with a purpose to laud credit money to the needy nations. It was decided to allow India to appoint the Indian Chairman of the said bank. It all added the prestige and honour of India in the international field.

In a major victory for India at international forum, 6th BRICS Summit agreed to establish the new development bank. Shanghai was selected as the headquarters, first president of the bank will be an Indian. PM Narendra Modi stressed, the bank would benefit not only the member-nations but also the developing world.

Narendra Modi government plans to call for a SAARC bank in the lines of BRICS bank to take forward its South Asia initiative. The proposed bank could give a boost to economic development of SAARC nations—Afghanistan, Bangladesh, Bhutan, India, Maldives, Nepal, Pakistan and Sri Lanka.

Bibliography

Allardt, E and S Rokkan (eds), *Mass Politics* (New York: The Free Press, 1970).

Allardt, E and Y Littunen (eds), *Cleavages, Ideologies and Party Systems* (Helsinki: Westermack Society, 1964).

Almond, GA and GB Powell, *Comparative Politics: A Developmental Approach* (New Delhi: Amerind Publishing Co, 1966).

Almond, GA and JS Coleman (eds), *The Politics of the Development Areas* (Princeton: University Press, 1960).

Andrews, CF and G Mukerji, *The Rise and Growth of the Congress in India* (London: George Allen & Unwin 1938).

Andrews, Charles Freer, *The Renaissance in India: Its Military Aspect* (London: Young People's Missionary Movement, 1912).

Apter, David E (ed) *Ideology and Discontent* (London: The Free Press of Glencoe, 1964).

Azad, Maulana Abul Kalam, *India Wins Freedom: An Autobiographical Narrative* (Bombay: Orient Longmans, 1959).

Bahuguna, Hemwati Nandan, *Indianising Whom?* (New Delhi: National Herald Press, 1970).

Baily, FG, *Tribe, Caste and Nation: A Study of Political Activity and Political Change in Highland Orissa* (Manchester: University Press, 1960).

Ball, AR, *Modern Politics and Government* (London: Macmillan, 1971).

Bharatiya Jana Sangh, *Bangla Desh: Recognition Delayed is Recognition Denied* (New Delhi: Navchetan Press, 1971).

Barker, Earnest, *Principles of Social and Political Theory* (Oxford: University Press, 1961).

Batra, Puran, *Political Parties in India: An Advanced Critical Study* (Agra: Navayug Sahitya Sadan, 1955).

Baxter, C, *The Jana Sangh: A Biography of an Indian Political Party* (Philadelphia: University of Pennsylvania Press, 1969).

Bell, D, *The End of Ideology* (Glencone: The Free Press, 1960).

Berry, David R, *The Sociology of Grass Roots Politics: A Study of Party Membership* (London: Macmillan, 1970).

Bharatiya Jana Sangh: Principles and Policy (New Delhi: Jana Sangh).

Bharatiya Jana Sangh: Resolution of the Eighth Annual Session and the Working Committee, Nagpur, 23-25 January 1960 (Delhi: Raj Art Press, 1969).

Bharatiya Jana Sangh Ka Chunav Ghosna Patra (New Delhi, Jana Sangh, 1956).

Bharatiya, Jana Sangh, Ninth Annual Session, 30-31 December 1960 and January 1961 Annual Report (New Delhi: Navchetan Press).

Bharatiya Jana Sangh Presidential Address, Bharatiya Pratinidhi Sabha Session, Gwalior, 11-15 August 1964 (New Delhi: Navchetan Press).

Bharatiya Jana Sangh Resolutions, Fifteenth All India Session, 25-27 April 1969, Bombay (New Delhi: Navchetan Press).

Bharatiya Jana Sangh Resolution passed by Bharatiya Karya Samiti, 18-19 March 1972, New Delhi (New Delhi: Navchetan Press).

Bharatiya Jana Sangh Resolution passed by the All India Working Committee, Rajahmundry (Andhra Pradesh), 29-30 September and October 1962 and emergent meeting at Delhi on 1 November 1962 (New Delhi: Navchetan Press).

Bharatiya Jana Sangh Resolutions of the Bharatiya Pratinidhi Sabha and the Working Committee, Varanasi, 12-15 November 1961 (Delhi: Raj Art Press).

Bharatiya Jana Sangh Resolutions of the Bharatiya Pratinidhi Sabha, Delhi, 11-12 August 1963 (New Delhi: Navchetan Press).

Bharatiya Jana Sangh Resolutions passed at the Seventh Annual Session, 26-28 December 1958, Bangalore (Delhi: Arjun Press, 1958).

Bharatiya Jana Sangh Resolutions passed by All India Working Committee at Raipur on 1-4 July 1969 and New Delhi on 30-31 August and 1 September 1969 (New Delhi: Navchetan Press).

Bharatiya Jana Sangh Resolutions passed by Bharatiya Karya Samiti on 10-

11 July 1965, Jabalpur, Madhya Pradesh (New Delhi: Navchetan Press).

Bharatiya Jana Sangh Resolutions passed by Bharatiya Karya Samiti, New Delhi, 15 March 1971; Bharatiya Pratinidhi Sabha Session, Udaipur, 3-4 July 1971 and Bharatiya Arya Samiti, New Delhi, 13 August 1971 (New Delhi: Navchetan Press).

Bharatiya Jana Sangh Resolutions passed by the Bharatiya Karya Samiti (All India Working Committee) at Patna on 22-23 April 1961 (Delhi: Raj Art Press).

Bharatiya Jana Sangh Resolutions passed by the Bharatiya Karya Samiti, Patna, 4-6 December 1964 (Delhi: Arjun Press).

Bharatiya Jana Sangh Resolutions passed by the Bharatiya Karya Samiti, Jaipur, 3-4 April 1965 (New Delhi: Navchetan Press).

Bharatiya Jana Sangh Working Committee Resolutions, New Delhi, 6-7 April 1963 and Prayag, 13-14 June 1963 (New Delhi: Navchetan Press, nd).

Bharatiya Jana Sangh, *Constitutions and Rules* (New Delhi: Jana Sangh, 1972).

Bharatiya Jana Sangh Resolutions passed at the Tenth All India Session, Bhopal, 29-31 December 1962 and at emergent Working Committee meeting on 19-20 January 1963 (Delhi: Arjun Press).

Bharatiya Jana Sangh, *Integrate Kashmir: Mukherjee-Nehru and Abdullah Correspondence*.

Bharatiya Jana Sangh Election Manifesto, 1962 and 1967.

Bharatiya Jana Sangh, *Economic Policy Resolutions of Bharatiya Jana Sangh* (Bombay: Rajmundra, 1969).

Bimla, Prasad, *The Origins of India's Foreign Policy* (Calcutta, Bookland, 1960).

Binder, L, *Religion and Politics in Pakistan* (Berkeley: University of California Press, 1961).

Blackham, HJ, *Political Discipline in a Free Society* (London: George Allen & Unwin, 1961).

Indian National Congress, Bombay, *Economic Policy Resolution and Follow-up Measures* (New Delhi: National Herald Press, 1970).

Bondurant, JV, *Regionalism Versus Provincialism: A Study in Problems of India National Unity* (Berkeley: University of California Press, 1958).

Braibanti, R and JJ Spengler (eds), *Tradition, Values and Socio-Economic Development* (Durham NC: Duke University Press, 1961).

Brass, PR, *Factional Politics in an Indian State: The Congress Party in Uttar Pradesh* (Berkeley: University of California Press, 1965).

Brecher, Michael, *India's Foreign Policy* (New York, 1957).

_______, *The Struggle for Kashmir* (Toronto: Ryerson Press, 1953).

Bright, JS, *Guruji Golwalkar and RSS* (Delhi: New India Publishing Co).

_______, *Hindu Code Bill—Will it Kill the Congress* (Delhi: New India Publishing Co, 1950).

Brown, WN, *The United States and India and Pakistan* (Cambridge: Harvard University Press, 1953).

Brzezinski, Z, *Ideology and Power in Soviet Politics* (New York: Praeger, 1962).

Burger, AS, *Opposition in a Dominant Party System* (Bombay: Oxford University Press, 1969).

Burks, RV, *The Dynamics of Communism in Eastern Europe* (Princeton: University Press, 1961).

Callard, KB, *Pakistan's Foreign Policy* (New York: Institute of Pacific Relations, 1959).

Constitution of the Communist Party of India (Cochin: Communist Party Publication, 1971).

Cantril, H, *The Politics of Despair* (New York, Basic Books, 1958).

Cassinelli, EW, *The Politics of Freedom* (Washington: University of Washington Press, 1961).

Chandidas, Morehouse, Clark, Fontera (eds), *India Votes: A Source Book on Indian Elections* (Bombay: Popular Prakashan, 1968).

Chao, Kuo-Chun, *The Mass Organization in Communist China* (Cambridge: MIT Centre for International Studies, 1953).

Chatterjee, B, India: *The Congress Splits* (Delhi, S Chand & Co, 1971).

Chaube, S (ed), *Syama Prasad Smarika* (Calcutta: Swastik Mudranalaya, 1959).

Chhabra, HS, *Opposition in the Parliament* (Delhi, New Publishers, 1953).

Congress Bulletin, April-May 1969 (Delhi: Printsman).

Congress Bulletin, June-July 1969 (Delhi: Printsman).

Congress on Communalism (New Delhi: The Master Printers).

Congress Seva Dal: *Organisation and Working* (Delhi: Rajesh Printing Press, 1972).

Congress Seva Dal: *Questions and Answers for Workers* (Delhi: Rajesh Printing Press, 1972).

Curran, Jean Alonzo, *Militant Hinduism in Indian Politics: A Study of the RSS* (New York: Institute of Pacific Relations, 1951).

Dahl, RA, *Modern Political Analysis* (New Delhi: Prentice-Hall of India, 1965).

Dahrendorf, R, *Class and Class conflict in Industrial Society* (London, Routledge and Kegan Paul, 1959).

Dange, SA, *India from Primitive Communism to Slavery: A Marxist Study of Ancient History in Outline*, 4th edition (New Delhi People's Publishing House, 1961).

Das, Durga, *India: From Curzon to Nehru and After* (London: Collins, 1969).

Das, Pitambar, *Party Education Series Grade I Course*, Bharatiya Jana Sangh Presidential Address Eighth Annual Session, Raghuji Nagar, Nagpur, 23-25 January 1960 (Delhi: Raj Art Press).

Deo, S, *The New Congress* (New Delhi, AICC, 1949).

Desai, AR, *Social Background of Indian Nationalism* (Bombay: Popular Book Depot, 1959).

Dhawan, G, *The Political Philosophy of Mahatma Gandhi* (Ahmedabad: Navajivan Publication House, 1951).

Dhebar, UN, *The Role of Panchayats in New India* (New Delhi: INC, 1957).

Dogra, Pandit Prem Nath, Presidential Address, Third Annual Session of Bharatiya Jana Sangh, Jodhpur, 30 December 1954 (Delhi: Arjun Press).

Downs, A, *An Economic Theory of Democracy* (New York: Harper, 1957).

Druhe, David N, *Soviet Russia and Indian Communism* (New York: Bookman Associates, 1959).

Dutt, RP, *The Indian Elections* (Bombay: People's Publishing House, 1952).

Duverger, M, *Political Parties: Their Organisation and Activity in the Modern State* (New York: John Wiley, 1963).

———, *Party Politics and Pressure Groups* (London: Nelson, 1972).

Easton, David, *The Political System* (New York: Alfred A Knopf, 1953).

Ebenstein, W, *Great Political Thinkers: Plato to the Present* (New York: Holt, Rinehart and Winston, 1963) 3rd edition.

Einavdi, M and F Goguel, *Christian Democracy in Italy and France* (Notre Dame, Indiana: University of Notre Dame Press, 1952).

Elders, Veld, SJ, *Political Parties: A Behavioural Analysis* (Bombay, Vora and Co Publishers, 1971).

Election Manifesto 1967 (New Delhi: Gulabsons Offset Works).

Election Manifesto 1971 (New Delhi: Yagti Jot Press).

Elenjimittan, A, *The Philosophy and Action of the RSS for Hind Swaraj* (Bombay: Laxmi Publication, 1951).

Emerson, R, *From Empire to Nation: The Rise to Self-Assertion of Asian and African People* (Cambridge: Harvard University Press, 1960).

Face the Facts: Recent Communal Riots (New Delhi: Navchetan Press, 1970).

Farguhar, JN, *Modern Religious Movements in India* (New York: Macmillan, 1915).

Farooqi, M, *Indian Muslims: Problems and Trends* (New Delhi: The New Age Printing Press, 1972).

Ferguson, JP, *Kashmir* (London: Centaur Press, 1961).

Follow-Up Measures After Bank Nationalisation (New Delhi: The New Statesman Press, 1970).

Friedrich, Carl and ZK Brzezinski, *Totalitarian Dictatorship and Autocracy* (Cambridge: Harvard University Press, 1956).

Friedrich, Carl J, *Constitutional Government and Democracy* (New Delhi: Oxford & IBH, 1974).

General Election Report, Bharatiya Pratinidhi Sabha Session, Kota, 26-27 May 1962 (New Delhi: Navchetan Press).

General Election Report, 1962-1967 (Bharatiya Jana Sangh, Delhi).

Ghosh, Deva Prasad, Presidential Address, Bharatiya Jana Sangh Sixth Annual Session Ambala (Punjab), 4-6 April 1958 (New Delhi: Navchetan Press).

Ghosna Patra, Bharatiya Jana Sangh (New Delhi: Jana Sangh, 1951).

Golwalkar, Madhav Sadashiv, *We or Our National Defined* (Nagpur: Bharat Publications, 1945).

Gopalaswami, RA, *Indian Polity: A Plea for Reform* (Bombay: Nachiketa Publications, 1970).

Greenleaf, WH, *Oakeshott's Philosophical Politics* (London: Longman, Green and Co, 1966).

Greenstein, FI, *The American Party System and the American People* (Englewood Cliffs Prentice-Hall, 1970), 2nd edition.

Gupta, B, *25 Years of Independence and the Challenge of the Path* (New Delhi: The New Age Printing Press, 1972).

Gupta, JBD, *Indo-Pakistan Relations, 1947-1955* (Amsterdam: Djambatan, 1958).

Haithcox, JP, *Communism and Nationalism in India: MN Roy and Comintern Policy, 1920-1939* (Princeton: University Press, 1971).

Hanham, HJ, *Elections and Party Management* (London: Longmans, Green and Co, 1959).

Harrison, Selig S, *India: The Most Dangerous Decades* (Princeton: University Press, 1960).

Hartmann, Horst, *Political Parties in India* (Meerut: Meenakshi Prakashan, 1971).

Hodgkin, TL, *African Political Parties: An Introductory Guide* (Harmondsworth: Penguin Books, 1961).

Hofstadter, Richar, *The Idea of Party System* (Calcutta: Scientific Book Agency 1972).

Indian National Congress Report of the General Secretaries (New Delhi: Maharashtra Press).

Indian National Congress, Constitution of the Indian National Congress as amended at the Bangalore Session of the AICC on 11 July 1968 (New Delhi: Sharma Offset Press, 1970).

Jain, JC, *The Murder of Mahatma Gandhi* (Bombay: Chetana, 1961).

Jana Sangh Declares *War on Poverty*, Election Manifesto (New Delhi: Radha Press 1971).

Jana Sangh on Bank Nationalisation (New Delhi: Navchetan Press).

Jana Sangh: *The Only Alternative, Election Manifesto* (New Delhi: Navchetan Press, 1972).

Jennings, WI, *Party Politics* (Cambridge: University Press, 1960).

Jhangiani, MA, *Jana Sangh and Swatantra—A Profile of the Rightist Parties in India* (Bombay: Manaktalas, 1967).

Jupp, James, *Political Parties* (London: Routledge and Kegan Paul, 1968).

K Sachidanand Murty, *Indian Foreign Policy* (Calcutta, Sadhana, 1964).

Kabir, Humayun, *Congress Ideology* (New Delhi: AICC, 1951).

Kamal, KL, *Party Politics in an Indian State: A Study of the Main Political Parties in Rajasthan* (New Delhi: S Chand and Company).

Karnik, VB (ed), *4th General Elections: Problems and Policies* (Bombay: Lalvani Publishing House, 1967).

Karunakaran, KP (ed), *Modern Indian Political Tradition* (New Delhi, Allied Publishers, 1962).

Karunakaran, KP, *India in World Affairs, August 1947–January 1950* (Calcutta: Oxford University Press, 1952).

Kashyap, SC (ed), *Elections and Electoral Reforms in India* (New Delhi: The Institute of Constitutional and Parliament Studies, 1971).

Kautsky, JH (ed), *Political Change in Under-Developed Countries: Nationalsim and Communism* (New York: John Wiley & Sons, 1962).

Kautsky, JH, *Moscow and the Communist Party of India: A Study in the Post-War Evolution of International Communist Strategy* (New York: John Wiley & Sons, 1956).

Kerala Mid-Term Election 1970—An Analysis (New Delhi: National Hearld Press, 1970).

Key, VO, Jr, *Politics, Parties and Pressure Groups* (New York: Thomas Y Crowell Company, 1956).

Kochahser, W, *The Politics of Mass Society* (Glencoe: The Free Press, 1959).

Kochanek, SA, *The Congress Party of India: The Dynamics of One Party Democracy* (Princeton: University Press, 1968).

Kothari, Krishna, Roy, Sheith, Shah, Ahmed and Maru (eds), *Party System and Election Studies* (New Delhi: Allied Publishers, 1967).

Kothari, Rajni, *Politics in India* (New Delhi: Orient Longmans, 1970).

Kumaramangalam, SM, *Constitutional Amendments: The Reason Why* (New Delhi: The National Herald Press, 1971).

La Palombara, J (ed), *Bureaucracy and Political Development* (Princeton: The University Press, 1963).

La Palombara, J and Weiner, *Political Parties and Political Development* (Princeton: The University Press, 1966).

Lane, RE, *Political Ideology* (New York: The Free Press, 1962).

Laski, Harold K, *Parliamentary Government in English* (London: George Allen & Unwin, 1938).

Lasswell, HD and Daniel Lerner, *World Revolutionary Elites* (Cambridge Mass: MIT Press, 1965).

Leiserson, A, *Parties and Politics: An Institutional and Behavioural Approach* (New York: Alfred A Knopf, 1958).

Lipset, SM, *Political Man: The Social Basis of Politics* (New York: Double-Day, 1960).

Lowi, Theodore, J, *The Politics of Disorder* (London: Basic Books, INC, Publishers, 1971).

Madhok, B, *Kashmir Problem: A Story of Bangling* (Delhi: Bharatiya Sahitya Sadan, 1952).

Madhok, Balraj, "India's Foreign Policy: The Jana Sangh View", *India Quarterly* (New Delhi), Vol XXIII, No 1, January 1967.

Madhok, Balraj, *Kashmir: Centre of New Alignments* (Delhi, Deepak, 1963).

Madhok, Balraj, Presidential Address at the Bharatiya Pratinidhi Sabha Session (General Council Session), Nagpur, November 3-6, 1966, Bharatiya Jana Sangh, Delhi (New Delhi: Navchetan Press).

Malhotra, AS, *Communism Today No 4: What is the Communist Party?* (New Delhi: The New Age Printing Press, 1970).

Malkani, KR, *The Rise and Fall of the Congress* (Delhi: Vijay Pustak Bhandar, 1951).

Masani, MR, *The Communist Party of India* (New York: Macmillan, 1954).

Mehrotra, SR, *The Emergence of the Indian National Congress* (Delhi: Vikas Publications, 1971).

Mekenzie, R, *British Political Parties* (London: Mercury Books, 1963).

Michels, R, *Political Parties: A Sociological Study of the Oligarchical Tendencies of Modern Democracy* (translated by Eden Paul and Cedar Paul (New York: Dover Publications 1959).

Morris-Jones, WH, *The Government and Politics of India* (London: Hutchinson, 1964).

Mukherjee, S, *Who Really Aids India, USA or USSR?: A Study in Contrast of Economic Assistance* (New Delhi: The New Age Printing Press, 1972).

Nanda, G, *Progress of Land Reforms in India* (New Delhi, INC, 1957).

Narain, Iqbal, *Twilight or Dawn: The Political Change in India, 1967-71* (Agra: Shiv Lal Agarwala and Company, 1972).

Narayan, S, *Towards a Socialist Economy* (New Delhi: INC, 1956).

Nehru, Jawaharlal, *Independence and After: A Collection of Speeches, 1946-1949* (New York: The John Day Company, 1950).

Neumann, S (ed), *Modern Political Parties* (Chicago: The University Press, 1956).

Nizami, TA, *The Communist Party and India's Foreign Policy* (New Delhi: Associated Publishing House, 1971).

Ostgrogorski, NI, *Democracy and the Organisation of Political Parties* (London: Macmillan, 1902).

Palmer, ND, *The Indian Political System* (Boston: Houghton Mifflin Company, 1961).

Park, RL and I Tinker (eds), *Leadership and Political Institution in India* (Princeton: Princeton University Press, 1959).

Patel, SR, *Foreign Policy of India* (Bombay, Tripathy, 1960).

People Victory: An Analysis of 1971 Elections (New Delhi: National Herald Press, 1971).

Peoples Victory Second Phase: An Analysis of the 1972 General Elections to State Assemblies (New Delhi: National Herald Press, 1972).

Plamenatz, J, *Ideology* (London: Pall Mall, 1970).

Political Report and Political Resolution (New Delhi, CPI, 1971).

Prasad, RC, *Democracy and Development: The Grass Roots Experience in India* (Delhi: Rachna, 1971).

———, *The Mature Electorate* (New Delhi: Ashish Publishing House, 1975).

Presidential Address at the Thirteenth All India Session, Jullundur (Punjab), 30 April–2 May 1966, Bharatiya Jana Sangh (New Delhi: Navchetan Press).

Presidential Address Bharatiya Jana Sangh Eleventh Annual Session, Ahmedabad, 28-30 December 1963 (Lucknow: Swadesh Press).

Presidential Address Bharatiya Jana Sangh Seventh Annual Session, 26-28 December 1958, Class House, Lalbagh, Bangalore (Bangalore: Kesari Press).

Purohit, BR, *Hindu Revivalism and Indian Nationalism* (Sagour: Sathi Prakashan, 1965).

Raj, KN, *Indian Economic Growth: Performance and Prospects* (Delhi: The National Printing Works, 1965).

Rajan, MS (ed), *Studies in Politics* (Delhi: Vikas Publications, 1971).

Rao, MVR, *A Short History of the Indian National Congress* (New Delhi: S Chand & Co, 1959).

Rao, A Rama, Bharatiya Jana Sangh Presidential Address, Bharatiya Pratinidhi Sabha Session, Kota (Rajasthan), 26-27 May 1962 (New Delhi: Navchetan Press).

Report of the General Secretaries, December 1969–May 1970 (New Delhi: National Herald Press).

Report of the General Secretaries, June 1970–September 1971 (New Delhi: National Herald Press, 1971).

Report of the General Secretaries, October 1971–May 1972 (New Delhi: National Hearald Press, 1972).

Resolution on Economic Policy and Programme passed by the AICC at its meeting in July 1969 in Bangalore (New Delhi: National Herald Press).

Resolutions adopted by the Bharatiya Pratinidhi Sabha and the Bharatiya Karya Samiti of Bharatiya Jana Sangh, Poona, 27 June to 8 July 1959 (New Delhi: Arjun Press, 1959).

Resolutions passed at the Bharatiya Pratinidhi Sabha Session (General Council) and the Working Committee, Hyderabad, 27-28 August 1960 (Delhi: Raj Art Press, 1960).

Resolutions passed by the Bharatiya Karya Samiti (Working Committee) on 30 June and 1-2 July 1967, Simla (New Delhi: Navchetan Press).

Resolutions passed by the Bharatiya Pratinidhi Sabha and Working Committee at Kota, 24-27 May 1962 (Delhi: Navchetan Press).

Roland Yound, *Approaches to the Study of Politics* (Evaustan III: North-Western University Press, 1962).

Rules of the Indian National Congress framed under Article VIII(f)(i) and other articles of the constitution in force from 27 December 1969 (New Delhi: Printsman).

Sahni, NC, *Coalition Politics in India* (Jalandhar: New Academic Publishing Company, 1971).

Sharma, SD, *Congress Approach to International Affairs* (Delhi: The Everest Press, 1972).

Shklar, JN (ed), *Political Theory and Ideology* (New York: Macmillan, 1966).

Simla Surrender (New Delhi: Navchetan Press).

Singh, Mahendra P, *Cohesion in a Predominant Party: The Pradesh Congress and Party Politics in Bihar* (New Delhi, S Chand & Co, 1975).

Sirsikar, VM, *Political Behaviour in India: A Case Study of the 1962 General Elections* (Bombay: Manaktalas, 1965).

Sondhi, ML, *Wanted—A National Foreign Policy* (New Delhi: Navchetan Press, 1968).

Swamy, S, *Nuclear Policy for India* (New Delhi: Navchetan Press, 1968).

Text of Speech at All India Conference of Peace and Solidarity, Calcutta, 20 September 1972 (New Delhi: Everest Press, 1972).

The Message of Mahatma Gandhi (Delhi: Everest Press).

Tinker, H, *India and Pakistan: A Political Analysis* (New York: Frederick A Praeger, 1962).

Upadhyaya, Deendayal, *Political Diary* (Bombay: Jaico Publishing House, 1968).

Upadhyaya, Deendayal, Bharatiya Jana Sangh Presidential Address,

Fourteenth Annual Session, Shri Narain Nagar, Calicut, 28-30 December 1967 (New Delhi: Navchetan Press).

Vajpayee, Atal Bihari, Bharatiya Jana Sangh Presidential Address, Bharatiya Pratinidhi Sabha Session, Indore, 8 September 1968 (Indore: Modern Printers).

Vajpayee, Atal Bihari, *Simla Samjhota 'Maidan Me Jite—Mej Par Hare'* (New Delhi: Bharatiya Jana Sangh Publication, 1972).

Varma, VP (ed), *A Study of the Mid-Term Elections in Bihar, 1969*, (Patna: Institute of Public Administration, PU, 1970).

Weiner, M, *Party Politics in India: The Development of Multi-Party System* (Princeton: The University Press, 1957).

Weiner, and Kothari (eds), *Indian Voting Behaviour Studies of the 1962 General Elections* (Calcutta: Firma KL Mukhopadhyaya, 1965).

Index